Future Visions for U.S. Defense Policy

Four Alternatives

Presented as

Presidential Speeches

John Hillen, Project Director

A Council Policy Initiative

Sponsored by the Council on Foreign Relations

CONTENTS

FOREWORD

In 1997, the Council on Foreign Relations launched a series of *Council Policy Initiatives* (CPI) whose purpose is to encourage interested Americans to debate key international issues.

We do so by:

1. Choosing topics of major importance. This year's topics are defense and trade.

2. For each topic, convening a panel of experts to decide on major policy alternatives. These experts prepare substantive background papers on each of the choices.

3. Turning the background papers over to a professional speechwriter, who works them into easily understandable speeches a president or cabinet official could give to the interested public.

4. Publishing a volume that contains these speeches plus a cover memo as if written by a key presidential adviser.

5. Sponsoring a nationally televised debate from New York or Washington and regional meetings around the country.

The Council takes no institutional position on the CPI subjects. Our aim is simply to make the best case for each alternative.

Special thanks are due to Project Director John Hillen, the Council's Olin Fellow for National Security Studies, and Susan Tillou, research assistant for the project. Our speechwriter, Harvey Sicherman, also deserves kudos. John Hillen and I wrote the "Memorandum to the President from the National Security Adviser."

We are delighted to launch our Council Policy Initiatives program with this defense project. As good as it is, we hope to do even better as we go along.

Leslie H. Gelb
President

ACKNOWLEDGMENTS

The Council's Defense Policy Review was based on the work of several analysts. It was then subjected to peer reviews by experts in many different areas, from diverse fields and backgrounds, and holding many different viewpoints. The core team consisted of:

Project Director and Speech Editor:	John Hillen, *Council on Foreign Relations*
Chief Speechwriter:	Harvey Sicherman, *Foreign Policy Research Institute*
National Security Adviser Memorandum Writers:	John Hillen, *Council on Foreign Relations* Leslie H. Gelb, *Council on Foreign Relations*
Consulting Analysts:	Michael O'Hanlon, *The Brookings Institution* Michael Vickers, *Center for Strategic and Budgetary Assessments* Carl Conetta (with Charles Knight), *Project on Defense Alternatives, Commonwealth Institute*
Research Associate:	Susan Lynne Tillou, *Council on Foreign Relations*

The project director would like to thank the many individuals who graciously contributed to this project. In addition to benefiting from the work of the consulting analysts, the Council drew heavily on comments from Council staff, especially Morton H. Halperin, Richard Betts, Michael Peters, and Gideon Rose as well as the Council's 1997–98 military fellows, Colonels George Flynn (USMC) and Frank Klotz (USAF).

The Council enlisted the advice of over 100 former defense officials and intellectuals, many of whom provided very detailed feedback. We regret that the nature of the project prohibited us from using every point of advice, but we tried to honor as many as possible. The Council also held two meetings in Washington, where the ideas behind the speeches and early drafts of the speeches themselves were vetted. Attendance at the meetings by no means implies agreement with the ideas or statements contained herein, but the comments and criticisms made at the meetings were invaluable. The attendees were:

JULY 24, 1997, MEETING

Stephen A. Cambone, *Center for Strategic and International Studies*
Patrick Clawson, *Institute for National Strategic Studies*
Michele Flournoy, *Department of Defense*
Morton H. Halperin, *Council on Foreign Relations*
Kenneth M. Pollack, *The Washington Institute*
Gideon Rose, *Council on Foreign Relations*
John J. Shanahan, *Center for Defense Information*
Thomas E. Smith, *National War College*
Cindy Williams, *Congressional Budget Office*

OCTOBER 6, 1997, MEETING

Pauline H. Baker, *The Fund for Peace*
Ellen L. Frost, *Institute for International Economics*
Morton H. Halperin, *Council on Foreign Relations*
Fred C. Ikle, *Center for Strategic and International Studies*
Lawrence J. Korb, *The Brookings Institution*
Richard M. Moose, *The CNA Corporation*
Brent Scowcroft, *The Scowcroft Group*

Acknowledgements

Karen M. Sughrue, *Council on Foreign Relations*
Dov S. Zakheim, *SPC, Incorporated*

The project director would like also to thank April Wahles-
tedt and Lise Stone for their support and hard work throughout;
Karen M. Sughrue, Erika Burk, and Irina Faskianos for their coor-
dination of the national outreach effort; Alicia Werble de la
Campa, Arleen O'Brien, and Jan Murray for their development
help; and David Kellogg, Patricia Dorff, and Sarah Thomas for
their editorial and production assistance. Finally, the diligence,
patience, professionalism, and overall excellence of the work done
by Susan Tillou should be recognized as the key contribution in
the completion of this project.

We are grateful for the generous support of The Smith-
Richardson Foundation and the Ploughshares Fund, without
which this project would not have been possible.

MEMORANDUM TO THE PRESIDENT

FROM: "The National Security Adviser"

SUBJECT: Looking at the Threat Horizon and U.S. Military
Responses; Alternative Defense Policy Speeches

PURPOSE

There is no real pressure here at home to rethink or redo U.S. defense
policy, except perhaps from a dwindling community of defense intellectuals. Nor do external events compel us urgently to review
these matters. No strategic security gap exists. Current U.S.
forces, along with those of our allies and friends, seem sufficient
to reasonably safeguard America against presently foreseeable
threats.

But there are strong reasons to look ahead at this moment of
strategic calm. An economic crisis at home could ignite powerful demands for deep, immediate, and rash cuts in military spending. An international crisis, unique and unrepeatable, also could
erupt and force imprudent changes in military capabilities. For example, the Cuban missile crisis of 1962 drove both the United States
and the Soviet Union into a dangerous and taxing competition in
nuclear weapons. Now, we have time for more deliberate decisions.
It may well be that our present strategy of buying enough to
provide reasonable hedges against everything from regional wars
to specific responses to terrorism will leave us vulnerable to big-
ger regional threats than we can handle or to a major technological breakthrough by a potential adversary. Or we may be missing
a major opportunity to use this time of relative peace to forge new
institutions for collective defense. And if major new departures are

deemed necessary and advisable, we must make the key decisions now to build the kinds of forces we will require 10 to 20 years from now. Reshaping our forces takes a long time.

No one should tangle easily with the argument that if it ain't broke, don't fix it. But given all the changes enveloping the world since the collapse of the Soviet Union, and uncertain public moods in America, things could be broken right at or over the horizon. This memo is designed to look at that horizon and make the best cases for new defense policies. The memo provides background information and a comparative analysis of three alternative defense policies, as well as an assessment of present strategy. The memo is followed by four alternative speeches, each presenting a clear strategic thrust.

Prudent Defense: The United States has to be ready to meet the full range of threats from conventional war among major powers to peacekeeping operations. The problem is that our capability and readiness for doing so are gradually diminishing. To meet this problem, we have to upgrade our superiority almost across the board, more or less evenly divided between the services, including technological upgrades and greater reliance on allies for peacekeeping duties. This will require an increase in defense spending by some 10 percent.

Innovative Defense: Given our considerable overall military superiority against current and future rivals, the only challenge to that superiority comes from the chance that one or more of them could achieve a devastating breakthrough in military technology. To meet this challenge, we will need innovative technology to do most military missions with smaller and smarter forces, and with fewer casualties. Future wars, even more than in the past, will turn on applied technology, and we must focus defense dollars less on current readiness and more on keeping our technological superiority. We can do this without raising military spending and perhaps even see a slight reduction in the defense budget in future years.

Cooperative Defense: We are going to overload domestic circuits and alienate friends and allies if we continue either to assume responsibility and leadership for most international turmoil or fail to do so. This is the time to build international institutions and ad hoc coalitions for collective security, and focus them on the real new threat—civil and ethnic violence. By ridding ourselves of a wasteful and overly large Cold War military, we can reduce military spending by some 15 to 20 percent.

Balanced Defense: With so much uncertainty at home and abroad, it is impossible to rank threats to our national security. We should continue doing what we are doing—putting sufficient military muscle into being ready on as many fronts as possible. Defense spending should stay constant for the next 10 years—equivalent in today's dollars to $250 billion per year.

We give you the above alternatives in speech form so you can get a feel for making the case to the public. Although the speeches are not written *for* experts, they are written *by* experts, and obviously you and your speechwriters would need to scrub the presentation. Each speech is also two-dimensional, in a sense. Each gives a more or less pure direction or thrust. The aim of the purity is to clarify your choices. Obviously, in final form you could mix, match, and blend the choices somewhat.

Other caveats about the speeches are listed later in this memo, but one must be highlighted here. They provide no overall foreign or national security context. Thus, they do not discuss critical questions such as which international problems are better dealt with by means other than military power, certainly initially at least. Nor do the speeches dwell on the critical relationships between force, diplomacy, economic power, and the like. Nor is there much discussion of allies and friends, who will play an important role in whatever we do. For the foreseeable future, almost all of them are cutting back their military capacity and seem even more reluctant than Americans to undertake foreign military burdens. Still, the speeches address what a defense policy must address, namely, what kinds of forces we should develop and plan to use to meet likely military threats and to support a balanced and "internationalist" U.S. foreign policy.

U.S. Defense Policy

The United States currently has an unprecedented opportunity to review fundamental choices in its national security strategy and defense policy. In 1998, America faces no readily apparent major conventional military threats or likely nuclear threats. At the same time, there are some smaller yet still dangerous challenges from rogue states in key areas of the world and a host of emerging new security threats, such as weapons of mass destruction wielded by terrorists or rogue states, ethnic violence and refugee problems in failed or failing states, and the possibility of new forms of warfare such as information warfare or the use of biological weapons. This time of "strategic pause," coupled with the rise of new unconventional threats and technological potential, calls for a serious reexamination of U.S. defense strategy, force size and structure, weapon systems, deployments overseas, and the organization and workings of the Department of Defense (DOD).

Since 1991, DOD has completed three major defense policy reviews to address these questions: the Bush Base Force Review (1991), the Clinton administration's Bottom-Up Review (1993), and the congressionally mandated Quadrennial Defense Review (1997). In addition, two independent panels also mandated by Congress have undertaken comprehensive examinations of DOD's budget, force structure, strategy, deployment posture, and modernization program: the 1994–95 Commission on Roles and Missions of the Armed Forces and the 1997 National Defense Panel.

In general, as shown in table 1, the reviews have changed little besides matching smaller (but similar) force structures to a defense spending account that declined some 38 percent since 1985 before leveling off this year. In the absence of a clear strategy, such as that of the Cold War's containment strategy, DOD has done little beyond these "budget drills" to define the purposes and strategy of U.S. military forces. Moreover, although there are no clear and present security threats on the scale of the Cold War, there has been no shortage of recent challenges to American security for which we have used the military. U.S. forces have been frequently deployed in the past seven years for missions ranging from traditional

Table 1. U.S. Defense Policy Reviews

	Actual Force 1991	Bush Base Force Recommendations 1991	Bottom-Up Review 1993	Quadrennial Defense Review 1997
Army (Divisions)	19 Active* 16 Reserve**	14 Active* 8 Reserve**	11 Active* 5+ Reserve**	11 Active* 5 Reserve**
Air Force (Tactical Wings)	22 Active 12 Reserve	15 Active 11 Reserve	13 Active 7 Reserve	12+ Active 8 Reserve
Navy	528 Ships 15 Carriers***	450 Ships 13 Carriers***	346 Ships 12 Carriers***	300+ Ships 12 Carriers***
Marine Corps (Personnel)	194,000 Active 45,000 Reserve	159,000 Active 35,000 Reserve	174,000 Active 42,000 Reserve	172,200 Active 37,800 Reserve
Total Uniformed Personnel	2,130,000 Active 1,170,000 Reserve	1,640,000 Active 920,000 Reserve	1,450,000 Active 900,000 Reserve	1,360,000 Active 835,000 Reserve

* Accounts for separate brigades and regiments not organized into divisions.

** Accounts for separate brigades not organized into divisions, but does not include two cadre divisions.

*** Includes training carrier.

deterrence and war fighting (Korea, Kuwait) to humanitarian relief and peacekeeping operations (Somalia, Haiti, Rwanda, Bosnia). In all, U.S. forces have been used for unexpected contingency operations almost 50 times since the Soviet Union's fall. In addition, threats such as terrorism, the proliferation of weapons of mass destruction, international crime, and other global problems pose new challenges to American security for which military forces may be part of an appropriate response.

The 1993 Bottom-Up Review postulated that U.S. strategy should make combat readiness its priority and focus on the threats of "major regional conflicts" (MRC), such as those that might occur in Korea or the Persian Gulf. This review was heavily criticized for being excessively focused on near-term contingencies at the expense of long-term preparedness and modernization, for overestimating the potency of the threats in these regions at the expense of less conventional challenges, and for failing to adequately fund the force DOD maintained it must have to carry out the two-MRC strategy. In addition, between 1993 and 1997, the U.S. military found its greatest challenges outside the MRC contingencies—in multilateral interventions to aid troubled states such as Somalia, Haiti, and Bosnia.

The Quadrennial Defense Review (QDR) was mandated by Congress to connect more closely threats in the post–Cold War world with DOD strategy and funding. The QDR report, released in May 1997, kept the basic two-MRC strategy intact, added the need for DOD to prepare for and perform "smaller-scale contingencies" (SSC), such as that in Bosnia, and cut the total force by an additional 115,000 uniformed personnel while maintaining basically the same force structure. The independent National Defense Panel (NDP), also mandated by Congress to critique the QDR, provided an initial assessment of this latest defense review. The NDP argued that the QDR was overly focused on the near term (five to ten years), maintained the two-MRC strategy without adequate justification, added missions and cut spending without setting mission priorities, failed to connect strategy with programs and budgets, ignored some important strategic developments (such as the role of space), and paid little attention to allies and coalitions.

The NDP report itself, released in December 1997, did not specifically identify the principal military challenges of 2020 and beyond. The report did not "attempt to provide all the answers" but rather aimed to "stimulate a wider debate on our defense priorities." It recommended that a "transformation strategy" of military and national security structures, operational concepts and equipment, and DOD's key business processes be "accelerated." Specifically, the NDP identified new operational challenges likely to confront U.S. forces, such as the absence of access to forward bases, information attacks (i.e., a strike against computer or communications systems), war in space, deep inland operations, urban operations, and new forms of attacks against the U.S. homeland. The NDP criticized the amount of money currently planned to upgrade older weapon systems and suggested that innovative new technologies be exploited by the design and purchase of new weapons that emphasize stealth, speed, mobility, precision strike capability, and advanced automation. The Pentagon accepted the report as part of the debate but has no plans to undertake the recommendations of the panel.

Thus, almost a decade after the end of the Cold War and after several major policy reviews, the basic questions about U.S. defense policy remain unanswered: What are the real threats to American interests around the globe both now and over the next 15 to 20 years? How should the United States best prioritize these threats and prepare to protect interests in the near term and the future? What types of forces, weapons, military strategies, and levels of resources will be needed?

THE OPTIONS

Here are crucial warnings to keep in mind as you read the distilled discussion of the options below and the draft speeches that follow:

—The speech you would actually give to Congress or other similarly involved audiences would be more general than the speech drafts here provided. It would also likely blend various elements of several of the speeches. The secretary of defense would be responsible for providing greater rationale and detail.

—None of these alternative defense policies represents a fundamental shift in U.S. foreign policy. Each assumes that the United States will stay firmly engaged in global security affairs, continue to lead in its military alliances, and continue regularly to have American forces abroad on both temporary and long-term forward deployments. Options representing a major foreign policy shift or large increases or cuts in military spending were deemed unrealistic at this time and therefore were not considered. Thus, none of the choices here presented requires adding $60 to $80 billion to the defense budget to make the United States into a global policeman capable of exercising what has sometimes been called "benevolent hegemony"; or reductions of a similar magnitude that would signify a new isolationism, called by some "strategic independence." These alternatives have small but vocal constituencies across the political spectrum but are not now politically realistic strategies. The choices outlined here span the broad middle ground of possible options, and all offer different ways to support the same basic goals of U.S. foreign policy.

—Major changes in nuclear policy are discussed principally in the "Cooperative Defense" alternative, where they fit as part of a major reduction in traditional military forces. A national missile defense system is treated most seriously in the "Prudent Defense" alternative. These and other nuclear issues are being pressed by small albeit active groups of political leaders and defense intellectuals. One group still wants a major effort to develop a defense against missile attacks. You are doing a number of things to keep options open on this front, short of major new decisions. The second group argues for a determined and gradual elimination, or virtual elimination, of all nuclear weapons. We assume that you are still not ready to consider either of these departures.

—Finally, the alternatives do not delve into specialized, but very important, defense debates, such as improving procedures and policies for procuring military materiel or reorganizing the military services (i.e., to separate services for tactical aircraft, strategic nuclear forces, space, or information warfare). There are a lot of potential savings involved here—and even more bureaucratic and political grief.

The summary of each option below characterizes the chief challenges to our security and a plan to align our forces to meet those challenges. A brief explanation of the strengths, weaknesses, and political impact of each option follows.

OPTION ONE: A PRUDENT DEFENSE

Despite the many recent changes in the international security environment, the principal threats to our security are conventional wars in areas of vital interest, such as Europe, Asia, and the Persian Gulf. These major threats, while happening less frequently than smaller threats, must always remain our strategic focus. Simultaneously, we must be able to deal with peacekeeping, ethnic conflicts, terrorism, and other lesser operations, although in a much more careful way than before and not at the expense of our war-fighting capability. Experience also teaches that we need a margin against the unexpected and a force that is robust enough to win at a relatively low cost in American blood and treasure. Not much help can be expected from broader collective security arrangements that have failed of late, and even dependable allies are growing less capable of aiding the United States in large-scale combat missions like Desert Storm.

Current strategy and budgets are inadequate and threaten to leave the United States with a military that is underfunded to meet technological change, overstretched by peacekeeping and other peripheral operations, and unprepared to protect core interests from potentially larger threats. Unless we tailor our forces to meet major current operational challenges, conduct some peacekeeping, *and* fund technological advances, we face a potentially catastrophic failure of deterrence and fighting ability.

The solution is to refocus U.S. strategy on the deterrence of major threats in our areas of vital interest. This requires a slight increase in our forces, more procurement of new equipment (especially with an eye for technological innovation), a national missile defense system, less use of our forces in peacekeeping, and more reliance on our allies for troops in small regional missions. To do this, we need a 10 percent increase in the defense budget.

Strengths
- Provides a force robust enough to give us high confidence in our ability to deter or defeat current and future threats—foreseen or unforeseen;
- Fully funds a realistic modernization program to replace equipment stocks from the 1970s and 1980s;
- Solves problems such as the deterioration in readiness due to the high pace of current operations by a much smaller force.

Weaknesses
- Requires a 10 percent increase in defense spending during a time of relative peace, little clear and present danger, and an atmosphere of fiscal austerity;
- Reduces the U.S. role in peacekeeping and humanitarian relief operations and therefore decreases U.S. influence in these matters;
- Makes nontraditional threats such as ethnic violence or international crime a lesser priority;
- Possibly misses the potential and comparative advantage of achieving major technological breakthroughs at less cost, since modernization will be evolutionary and cost more later.

Political Impact
- In Congress, this approach is likely to be supported by a bipartisan coalition of post–Cold War "hawks." Congress has added (as much as 5 percent) to the defense budget in each of the past three years. But it is likely to be opposed by post–Cold War peacekeeping supporters, traditional "doves," and budget-conscious conservatives. However, the increased spending in this option is helped by the rapidly shrinking federal deficit, the possibil-

ity of a budget surplus, and the historically low levels of current defense spending.

• In the Pentagon, it is likely to be strongly supported by all the services, as it reaffirms traditional roles and adds to force structure and investment.

• Among the general public, support cannot be expected without vigorous presidential leadership that will clearly enunciate the problems caused by current strategy, present an urgent but realistic picture of possible military threats, and explain the coming expected budget crisis when program costs far exceed planned funding.

• Among our allies, a reduction in the number of U.S. ground troops for multinational peacekeeping-type operations will not be well received and will likely diminish our influence in these situations.

OPTION TWO: AN INNOVATIVE DEFENSE

The post–Cold War world is a time of lessened threats to U.S. interests and a time of great opportunity for experimentation and change. During this strategic pause we must prepare for the future. The chief threat to our security will be the emergence over time of military powers with the strength or technological prowess to challenge our Cold War–era military. Our forces are now designed to fight the last war when we are in the middle of a far-reaching technological revolution. We therefore could face a catastrophe if our weapons prove to be ineffective and our tactics obsolete. The spread of technology, the high cost of innovation, and the long lead time for modernization all require action now if we are to be safe later. The United States is overly prepared to meet diminishing current threats (North Korea, Iraq) and in danger of wasting the opportunity to stay ahead of future competitors.

The United States must act now to take full advantage of the "revolution in military affairs." An innovative and high-tech U.S. military force will be dramatically more effective by using a space-, sea-, air-, and ground-based network of sensors to pinpoint enemy forces and a similar network of precision-guided munitions to destroy them from long range. Exploiting new technologies and fielding a very different information-age force will not require an increase in spending but will require major changes in spending priorities and also drastic revisions in U.S. doctrine, strategy, and force structure. To accomplish such objectives under the current budget, the United States will have to accept some risk that its forces will not be able to handle all current contingencies. Allies, the United Nations, and other collective security groups would have to be called upon to do more, especially in costly peacekeeping interventions. These risks, however, are more than offset by the "edge" such a strategy will give the United States well into the future. Innovation should be restored to its traditional role as America's most decisive strength. Spending priorities would be readjusted so that there would be no increase in the defense budget, which could conceivably decline in 15 to 20 years.

Strengths
- Harnesses traditional American advantages in technology and innovation to provide a force that will ensure U.S. primacy against military threats for 50 years or more;
- Protects effectively against "new" threats such as information warfare, weapons of mass destruction, and ballistic missiles;
- Solves the dilemma of a slow modernization that could cost more and produce less in the long run, and is now affordable at current spending levels.

Weaknesses
- Reduces the U.S. role in many current operations, thus accepting the risk of such conflicts spreading out of control while transforming a much smaller force to meet future challenges;
- Generates considerable institutional instability in each of the services and the Pentagon, as old bureaucratic and organizational structures are challenged and supplanted by new ones;

- Produces a force that might be too specialized to be relevant to labor-intensive threats, such as low-intensity conflicts and peacekeeping and humanitarian relief operations;
- Increases U.S. reliance on reluctant allies for undertaking the lesser tasks of global security, such as regional peacekeeping and humanitarian operations.

Political Impact
- In Congress, this approach is likely to be supported by only a small number of defense thinkers willing to take risks on national defense. However, members can be moved on this, as it appears to satisfy the concerns of many constituencies who wish for a more effective defense without increased costs. Presidential leadership—to emphasize the small amount of current risk and huge future benefits—will be critical.
- In the Pentagon, it is likely to be supported most vigorously by the Air Force (because of the emphasis on space) and fairly well supported by the Marine Corps. Resistance will come from elements in the Navy (particularly the naval aviation community) and the Army.
- It will garner support from the defense industry and business, since much of the new military technology will be borrowed "off-the-shelf" from civilian high-technology firms.
- Among the general public, you can expect support if you use the Office of the President to provide inspiration, as was done with the space program of the 1960s. And similarly with the space program, public support will falter as expensive experiments and systems fail, which is inevitable. Also, the imperatives of the program would have to be constantly reinforced in the absence of an obvious threat (such as that which helped start and drive the space program).
- Allies are already falling steadily far behind the United States in adapting new technologies to the military and would be more unhappy. The new approach would aggravate the growing incompatibility between allied and U.S. forces.

OPTION THREE: A COOPERATIVE DEFENSE

As the past seven years have shown, the main security challenges will come from smaller ethnic and civil conflicts that do not threaten our vital national interests but do demand we take some military action to protect our concerns and values. As matters now stand, either the United States leads a military intervention in these situations or nothing happens. If we get involved, we run risks that might outstrip our interests. If we fail to involve ourselves militarily, we risk small conflicts burgeoning into larger ones or damaging our leadership role. This puts the United States in a situation where we are not sure what kind of forces to build—for peacekeeping-type operations or Gulf War–type combat—and leads to dangerous confusion. Our concept of national security and military strategy is still built around outdated concepts of state-to-state conflict, massive nuclear deterrence, and large conventional forces. Conflicts like that in Bosnia as well as economic, developmental, and environmental problems are more relevant to national security today than old Cold War thinking.

The United States must recast its Cold War forces and tailor them to the conflicts of today's world. But since the United States cannot do everything and because the United Nations is not capable of playing a major role in global security, America must lead in building the capabilities of regional organizations and creating informal networks of allies to intervene in these complex conflicts. At the moment, none of the regional institutions or the United Nations itself is ready to accept greater responsibility. Unless the United States develops the power to act elsewhere, the burden will always fall on Washington. Building collective security institutions and capabilities will be a long, controversial, and difficult process. But it must begin with a determined effort by the United States to forge political cohesion in old and new international organizations and to help develop the necessary military capabilities to intervene. In addition, an emphasis on preventive diplomacy and multilateral responses will reduce the need for large deployed U.S. forces. We would also build networks of mutual assurance through arms control agreements that allow the

United States to take the lead in greatly reducing nuclear arsenals and the proliferation of weapons of mass destruction. This approach, a new form of collective security, would lessen pressures on the U.S. military to do everything and thus allow us to cut defense spending by some 15 to 20 percent.

Strengths
- Realigns a Cold War defense policy and force structure with current threats and security challenges;
- Reduces defense spending to levels more consistent with current budget priorities;
- Allows the United States to shift resources to fight "new agenda" threats such as global warming, refugees, terrorism, and the like;
- Takes full advantage of multilateral cooperation and keeps the United States involved in peacekeeping-type operations without overcommitment.

Weaknesses
- Reduces the capability of rapidly conducting combat operations on the scale of Desert Storm or larger;
- Sends signals of retrenchment and possible isolation to allies and adversaries by reducing U.S. deployments and American forces stationed overseas;
- Increases U.S. reliance on uncertain allies and undependable international organizations for helping to protect U.S. national interests;
- Raises issues over the foreign command of U.S. troops in multilateral operations led by an ally.

Political Impact
- In Congress, this approach will be opposed by advocates on both sides of the aisle of strong U.S. military power who vehemently oppose greater reliance on the United Nations and other multilateral organizations and military operations not led or dominated by the United States. Budget cutters and supporters of humanitarian interventions will support this approach.

- In the Pentagon, all services will openly oppose the downgrading of U.S. capability.

- Nuclear initiatives will be resisted by many constituencies, although there is new support among former military and political leaders for movement on this issue.

- Among allies, some will welcome the multilateral spirit of this policy, while others will denounce the move as an American retreat from responsibility.

OPTION FOUR: A BALANCED DEFENSE

(A speech that challenges these three departures with an explanation of current policies and priorities.)

The essence of America's strategic problems is the need to juggle a variety of needs in a world filled with uncertainties at a time when increasing military expenditures seems politically unwise. It would be politically unsustainable at home, and it would undermine our position abroad, if the United States no longer had the capability to deter or win large conventional wars as in Korea or the Gulf. At the same time, we need to be able to play important roles in peacekeeping operations (i.e., doing everything from providing combat troops to simply helping with intelligence and logistics). We degrade our combat capabilities somewhat by involving ourselves in peacekeeping operations, but we have to make whatever trade-offs there are. Some of these small ethnic and civil conflicts could explode into larger ones more threatening to American interests. What is more, the forces we now have, forward deployed and here at home, can still prevail in any large conventional conflict. And portions of them can as well perform with effectiveness in lesser military operations such as in Bosnia. We cannot be sure which of these threats will truly challenge vital American interests in the future, so we have to be prepared for all of them. Regional military organizations, our allies, and the United Nations are simply unprepared and unwilling to be prepared to shoulder these burdens.

Thus, the United States has to continue with its current balanced capabilities to meet a wide variety of threats and uncertainties. We may be able to get away with smaller forces to deter or fight conventional wars while putting somewhat greater reliance on forming U.S.-led and allied-supported peacekeeping operations and the like. Our forces are and will remain potent across the board compared with all possible adversaries. The costs of keeping this capability are constant and sustainable.

Strengths
- Balances competing priorities among conventional military threats, the need for action in smaller contingencies such as Bosnia, and threats as varied as the proliferation of weapons of mass destruction and terrorism;
- Gleans savings from efficiency measures and uses the money to balance the readiness to fight with technological modernization priorities;
- Offers steady capabilities and policy for current U.S. defense policy.

Weaknesses
- Does not prioritize the threats or missions to the point where DOD has enough focus truly to dominate in any one area. Offers the possibility of being merely fair at many different missions;
- Leads ultimately to underfunding and suboptimal results in both maintaining readiness to fight and modernization;
- Does not clearly prepare for future threats that are different from current challenges;
- Depends on a very optimistic estimate of savings from base closings and efficiency measures in order to fund the current force. Underfunding problems are likely to continue.

Political Impact
- On Capitol Hill, in the Pentagon, among allies, and among the American public, most will be content to leave spending levels and policy where they are. Although there will always be vocal

dissenters, any major changes in defense policy and spending in a time of peace will be more controversial than maintaining the status quo.

RECOMMENDATION

Convene your senior national security advisers informally to review this memo. If the sense emerges that present defense policy will put the United States at significant future risks, direct the secretary of defense to prepare a new draft speech—with supporting studies—presenting the new approach.

SPEECH ONE: A PRUDENT DEFENSE

A plan to reduce the strain on small and underfunded U.S. military forces by increasing the size of the force, decreasing participation in some peacekeeping operations, refocusing U.S. strategy on deterrence and war fighting, investing in the technologies of the future, and adding to the budget

Members of Congress and My Fellow Americans:

Thank you for welcoming me to Capitol Hill this evening. I have decided to speak to this special joint session of Congress directly because the president's first responsibility, under the Constitution, is our national defense. Let me assure you that a crisis is not imminent. But decisions are. We do not face the threat of attack. We do face the need to act.

The end of the Cold War has given the United States a unique opportunity to win the peace and to encourage an international order that favors democracy and prosperity. But to achieve these objectives, we must be able not only to deter aggression but to deal with a range of other challenges in a highly uncertain world that I will describe tonight.

Until now, we have attempted to meet these challenges with a military force reduced by one-third from its Cold War size. Simultaneously, we have used our troops with increasing frequency in peacekeeping and other missions short of war. As a result of this policy, we are wasting too much effort on peripheral issues. We have been short-changing the future, spending too much on today's wrong-headed priorities and too little on tomorrow's necessities. Our defense strategy has lost its focus, and our troops are in danger of losing their essential skills.

The plan I am proposing tonight—a prudent defense—will set America on the right course once more. First, we will redirect our military's attention to the main issue, the deterrence of conflicts in Europe, Asia, and the Middle East that might threaten vital U.S. interests, and not to lesser missions better handled in a different way. Second, we will also make greater investments in advanced weapons and training so that our forces will be able to meet the challenges of the future. Third, we will give our military the resources they need, even though it will cost more. The fact of the matter is that the United States will continue to need large land, air, and sea forces to ensure our freedom. This is a premium we must pay, and we can certainly afford to pay it.

Our defense planning begins with the definition of our interests and how military forces can secure them. The lessons of the twentieth century have taught Americans that what we value most—our democratic freedoms—can be put at risk by aggression far from our shores. And it is not only democracy that can be put at risk. Our well-being here at home depends on vital trading relationships we have forged with Europe, Asia, and the Middle East and with our neighbors in the Americas. The world's economic progress depends upon a broad framework of security, and America's military forces are a vital component of this framework. U.S. troops do more than deter aggression; they also embody America's determination to work for a better world.

History teaches that prosperity and security are the necessary escorts of our freedom. We have therefore made enormous sacrifices in lives and treasure throughout our history to preserve our democracy and indeed to give democracy a fighting chance in the rest of the world. And in this we have succeeded. After two world wars, a third called the Cold War, and numerous other conflicts, our democracy is today secure and prosperous.

It would be most unwise, however, for Americans to take this security for granted. The post–Cold War peace has yet to be won, and the world remains a far too unsettled and even dangerous place. Let me cite just a few examples of what I mean.

In Europe, the dangers of the Cold War have given way to pervasive uncertainty. Russia is going through wrenching political and economic change in the wake of communism's collapse. We are engaged in the expansion of NATO, while the European Union has begun the process of accommodating new members. These are large investments in the future security and prosperity of Europe that also call for a constructive relationship with Russia, and such has been our objective. Yet we must be realistic. No one can forecast Russia's future course, and in the past we have often been surprised as Moscow veered sharply between reform and revolution, cooperation and conflict.

A similar caution should govern our policy in Asia, where the People's Republic of China is trying to transform the world's most populous nation. We hope that the current authoritarian government will give way in time to democracy, but my responsibility as president is to do more than hope. There are American interests that need to be safeguarded, especially the freedom of shipping lanes and the restriction of weapons exports to unfriendly nations. In 1996, I sent two aircraft carrier battle groups to the Straits of Taiwan when China threatened to disrupt Taiwanese elections. As that episode showed, even in times of peace a robust and well-trained American military provides a healthy deterrent against those who would seek to disrupt the peace. Good intentions and vigorous diplomacy will not always be enough in dealing with other great powers whose interests may at times conflict with ours.

Then there are the rogue states, those who still openly threaten the peace. American troops today face a North Korean regime on the brink of starvation and without allies. Yet this same government remains armed to the teeth, its troops poised to invade South Korea. In the Persian Gulf, Iraq still possesses enough military power to threaten its neighbors in the absence of U.S. air, sea, and land power. Iran, a supporter of terrorism, seeks nuclear and other weapons of mass destruction. Both are located in the Persian Gulf, whose resources are vital to U.S. and allied security. No one should doubt that such rogue states would commit aggression if the United States were thought incapable of preventing it. And, as we have seen in the continuing confrontation with Iraq, deterring these rogue states still requires that the United States have large and readily deployable forces whose primary duty is to go to war if necessary.

Another danger is the spread of weapons of mass destruction—nuclear, chemical, or biological—that might fall into the wrong hands and possibly be used against the United States itself. Nor can we ignore the savage civil wars, such as has occurred in Bosnia, that threaten to spill over borders, spreading chaos and desperation in their wake.

The uncertainties and dangers of these many challenges mean that we need a large and well-trained military prepared to deal with a broad range of contingencies, perhaps even simultaneously in more than one region. The world has profoundly changed since the end of the Cold War, and responding to the new threats posed by ethnic violence, terrorism, international crime, and failing states is now a part of our national security strategy. But the extent to which these new threats should drive the focus of our strategy has very much been oversold. Like many other turning points in history, the end of the Cold War witnessed many observers trumpet that this was the end of history and the end of conflict between the world's major powers, all of whom were now market-oriented and democratically leaning states. We were told that the military challenges of the post–Cold War world would not be akin to deterring the Soviet Union or even deterring Iraq and North Korea. The new military threats were like those of Somalia, Haiti, and Bosnia.

I must tell you, however, that after seven years of dealing with these issues, I believe that the new missions of our time are not so new and not so critical that they should cause the world's only superpower to lose focus on the most crucial tasks of its security. These are the tasks that only the United States can perform, the traditional missions that keep the major powers free from conflict and the major systems of the world functioning in good order.

Our priorities should be clear. Think of it this way: If worst came to worst and we failed to deal with a renewed Russian threat, an emerging Chinese challenge, or Iraqi or Iranian aggression in the Gulf, the very foundations of our security and prosperity would be shaken. If we deter trouble in these areas, however, we can also deal with other issues. If we cannot, a lot of other issues will not matter. That is why in Europe and in Asia, for example, U.S. forces, working with our allies in NATO and Japan, encourage Russia and

China to join an international community they opposed until very recently. Our forces there are like firefighters. Just because the fire has gone out, that is no reason to disband the fire department. The peace dividend is not a chance to do away with a military that effectively deters threats to global security. The peace dividend is peace—and we must work hard for it.

A robust and well-trained American military force is insurance against a major power threat, but it must also be capable of deterring rogue states, acting against terrorists, and supporting U.S. diplomacy in the world's trouble spots. To do all this, our troops must be trained to act in case deterrence fails, and that means to fight and to win wars. The American way of war gives every advantage to our troops by emphasizing the need to achieve a rapid and overwhelming victory. This will not always be achieved with the relative ease of Desert Storm, but it should forever be our goal. There is nothing heroic in deploying just enough American forces to ensure there is a stalemate or slugfest on the battlefield. As commander in chief, I can assure you that I will field fighting forces that are well-trained and large enough to win a decisive victory in any future conflict.

At the end of the Cold War, the United States fielded a superb military, ranging from a broad-based nuclear arsenal to large, highly trained conventional air, sea, and ground forces with global reach, all backed by an advanced industry and capable reserves. Expecting more peaceful times, we reduced our active forces by over one-third. But things have not worked out as expected. We have sent our soldiers, sailors, marines, and airmen on missions abroad on numerous occasions, more often, in fact, than during the Cold War—over 25 times in the last 5 years, compared with 14 times under President Bush and 16 times under President Reagan. Some missions have been humanitarian operations that were short, focused, and effective. Others, such as Somalia, began that way but turned into something else. In that country, as in Haiti and Bosnia, our troops have been used to keep the peace and to build nations. Some of these operations, such as Bosnia, have required a more prolonged and expensive effort then we anticipated when they started.

U.S. Defense Policy

Our desire to help carries a cost. All the emphasis on the here and now, on these complex operations that are neither war nor peace, is beginning to undercut our ability to deter major conflicts.

LOSS OF FOCUS

First, our military is losing its focus on war-fighting skills, the most essential skills of American defense. Peacekeeping operations put our troops into situations more akin to police work than soldiering. Seizing ground, taking the offensive, and defeating the enemy are out. Restraint, forbearance, caution, and diplomacy are in. Large numbers of our troops and officers are therefore gaining much experience in peacekeeping at the expense of their skill in war fighting. Being prepared to conduct warfare on the scale of Desert Storm requires a sense of urgency and focus at every level in our military training. We would like to think that peacekeepers are also equally trained for fighting wars, but this is simply not true. Extensive retraining is required to bring our troops on peacekeeping duty back to combat readiness. I would like to say that the results have been worth the risks, but I cannot. We have all had a lesson in how difficult it is to repair societies torn apart by civil war or to revive a sense of nationhood in peoples who have lost it. We have refocused a large part of our military effort on humanitarian missions whose outcome is temporary, fragile, or easily reversed.

HOLLOWING THE FORCE

Second, smaller forces used more often have taken our troops to the edge of endurance and beyond. That threatens a slow hollowing-out of our military. Let me explain what I mean by "hollow." The key to our military capability is the quality of our troops. Today Americans volunteer to defend our country; there is no draft, and I do not propose to reinstate one. But just consider what has happened to our volunteer army since 1989. The number of active-duty soldiers has decreased by 36 percent, the budget is down by 38 percent, and yet missions have increased 300 percent. We have got a much smaller force, and we are using it more, much more. What does this do to our troops and their families? Listen to what they are saying. An officer at a major base used these words, and I quote:

> The more you take down the force, while keeping the same level of operations, the harder the remaining force works, which means more people get out, which means the remainder works harder, which means more of them get out, and now you're in this death spiral, right into the ground.

Those are alarming words, but even more alarming was a veteran colonel's observation that "what broke the army in Vietnam was the stress on the noncommissioned officers. . . . The families said, 'Enough of this,' and they all got out."

We are already seeing shortages among Army sergeants, staff sergeants, captains, and majors. The Air Force has begun to lose experienced pilots at an unprecedented rate and will be short by several hundred this year. Extended overseas duty is taking its toll on our Navy, putting great pressure on family life. And too many units are undermanned during their training cycle. So people do not train together at full strength, and they do not gain the experience they need to work as a team. Less training and less effective training also means an increasing risk of tragic accidents. The result of it all is "creeping hollowness" in the words of one Army general. It happened before, 20 years ago. We must not let it happen again.

OBSOLESCENCE

Third, we have begun to risk the future quality of our force. We expected to live off the large equipment stocks left over from the Cold War for a long time. But unanticipated use of our military abroad, obsolete equipment, and reduced budgets have taken their toll. The defense industry itself has "downsized" in lockstep with our overall defense reductions. Meanwhile, we have had to finance operations out of the maintenance funds, and the maintenance funds out of the procurement budget. And, as I noted, the defense budget itself has dropped 38 percent. Not since the 1930s have we had a defense budget that took less of the gross domestic product or a smaller percentage of the federal government's expenditures than the current one.

Something had to give.

And something did.

We can fix operations and maintenance fairly quickly, but what we cannot fix quickly is the procurement of new equipment. That takes time, lots of time. Because the money used to buy new and replacement equipment has dropped by some 70 percent since 1985, we have stopped buying tanks and other weapons systems that have proven themselves in battle. We cannot afford nearly the number of ships we have plans to use in the future. Within the current budget, we will not be able to acquire about 40 percent of planned aircraft. By the year 2005, almost all of our tanks and planes will be older than the soldiers or airmen driving and flying them. In short, our modernization plans have been severely curtailed.

It is a bad time for us to be in such a fix. Everyday we experience in our own lives the extraordinary technological changes that affect virtually everything we do. A military revolution is also underway that we cannot afford to miss. This revolution promises a more effective defense, ranging from new antimissile systems to more precise detection of an enemy's location and rapid, sure-fire reaction. Such military revolutions have happened before, and you can ask the veterans of the Gulf War, for example, to compare their experience with their fathers' in Vietnam or their grandfathers' in World War II. We must investigate this revolution and invest in the military hardware, software, and skills to use it. Today we are not doing enough of that.

I want to assure you that over the short term there is no danger that we will be inferior to those who might challenge us. We still retain the edge given us by the investments of a previous generation. But I do want to tell you that we must look beyond today or even tomorrow. We cannot risk a trend that could give us an obsolete, underequipped force. We must make new investments now—but in a sensible way. We will not sacrifice the capabilities of our current force in a mad dash to invest heavily in yet-to-be-proven technologies. Instead, we will launch a concerted effort to modernize our forces while maintaining a large and well-prepared military for near-term threats.

A THREE-POINT PLAN

The time has clearly come for us to change our ways. I am therefore asking your support for a three-point plan, a truly prudent defense policy. This plan will restore the proper focus of our forces on deterrence and war fighting, make investments to meet the threats of the future, and give our military the size and resources it needs to do the job efficiently.

1. We Must Restore the Proper Focus.

Our overall military objective remains the same. We should do our utmost to deter war. But if war comes, then we must win with as few casualties as possible. Those who defend us must therefore be trained as their first duty to fight and win wars because ultimately that capability is our best assurance of keeping the peace. That means a force able to meet the potential challenges to our security, able, above all, to prevent aggression or the threat of aggression in Europe, Asia, and the Middle East. These are the areas where we are deployed forward, where our interests are vital. As I noted earlier, a failure to protect these interests would shake the very foundations of our security and prosperity. However unlikely it may seem at the moment, we must also be prepared to deal with a new Russian problem, a turn for the worse in China, or aggression by an Iraq, an Iran, a North Korea.

You may have heard of the current Pentagon strategy that focuses on the need for our forces to fight two major regional conflicts almost simultaneously. I do not believe that this strategy should be the alpha and the omega of American military efforts around the globe, but it is an important capability to have. However, given the smaller size of our military today, its increasing focus on peacekeeping and other humanitarian operations, and the declining defense budget, I am not convinced that today we actually have the capability to wage two regional conflicts simultaneously. The plan I propose tonight will restore to the military the tools for this capability and do so within a strategy that is refocused on deterrence and combat readiness. Such a strategy will not only allow America to respond effectively to the most serious threats but will deter them from arising in the first place.

A proper focus on the most serious potential threat also allows us to evaluate other, lesser problems. This is the place to say a word about peacekeeping and military interventions short of war, the activity that has increasingly preoccupied our forces. There will be times when we must use force short of war to protect those interests.

When we do intervene, however, common sense will be our guide. That means not risking the lives of our soldiers unless it truly serves our interests and that by doing so, we do not detract from our ability to undertake other, more important military operations. Common sense also tells us that each operation should have a clearly defined goal, decisive means of accomplishing the goal, and a gauge of success or failure. And we must be realistic about what we can and cannot achieve. No one should expect American military intervention to heal the rift between brother and brother in a civil war or to rebuild a nation unwilling to rebuild itself.

Ultimately, we must be the police of our own interests. Fortunately, these interests are also shared by many other nations. Although the majority of our allies abroad have cut defense spending by an even greater margin than we, they still make an important contribution to deterrence. They are also of crucial assistance in peacekeeping operations, as we have seen in the Balkans. Although the United States is the only power capable of projecting and sustaining significant combat power, our allies have an increasingly important role to play. There is neither reason nor necessity for the United States to supply the bulk of the ground forces, for example, in every such operation. Many of our allies, especially in Europe, have turned the focus of their militaries away from fighting wars and toward peacekeeping. We should take advantage, as was successfully done in Albania in 1997, of these differing capabilities by encouraging allies to take the lead in the smaller missions of regional security.

Experience teaches that there is no substitute for carefully coordinated collective efforts in the pursuit of common interests.

I am confident that under these circumstances, the Congress and the American people will be fully supportive of such operations. That support, in and of itself, is also a key condition for success. We know that. So do those who oppose us.

This is the time, too, to say a word about the United Nations. The United States has long been a supporter and advocate of the United Nations and its collective security responsibility. Here, too, we have had much recent experience. We can and should expect the United Nations to act as a forum for the discussion of security problems by the international community. But we cannot and should not expect the United Nations to substitute for regional alliances, such as NATO, in the practical management of military intervention.

2. We Must Invest in the Future.
The current military procurement budget should be substantially increased in order to obtain the weapons we need tomorrow and to develop the weapons we will need the day after tomorrow. That calls for more purchases of hardware and more investment in research and development. We must also pay special attention to what some have called the revolution in military affairs, both the new technologies and the new concepts of how to use them. These promise to give us swift and precise identification of an enemy's location and more accurate weapons to defeat him. Smaller American forces, equipped with these new technologies, may be able to wield as much firepower as the much larger formations that now make up our military. As we experiment with these innovations, our current organizations, our doctrine, and indeed even the military culture may be sharply challenged. We should have the courage and the resources to face up to these challenges even as we should recognize that there is never any "magic bullet" that will

solve every defense problem. And of this we can be certain: The United States is not the only country seeking to use technological change in the pursuit of military advantage.

A word about missile and space defense. America today is vulnerable to ballistic missile attack. The largest single incident of U.S. loss of life in the Gulf War came when an Iraqi Scud missile hit a U.S. troops barracks in Saudi Arabia and killed 28 soldiers. Unfortunately, seven years after that incident, and with cheap missile technology spreading rapidly throughout the world, no technologically sound overall missile defense system has yet been devised. I seek to increase to a level of $8 billion to $10 billion a year our spending on research, development, and the deployment of such a system. I will also increase spending on protection for space-based systems such as satellites that are increasingly vital for both civilian and military applications.

3. We Must Expand Both the Forces and Their Resources.
U.S. defense forces are clearly too small and too underfunded for what they need to do. At currently projected defense levels, if the United States had to fight a conflict on the scale of Desert Storm in 2002, over 85 percent of the active Army, the entire Marine Corps, and at least 66 percent of Air Force fighter aircraft and Navy carrier battle groups would be engaged. Little would be left for other emergencies. A military must plan and prepare for more than just the reasonable and the expected—prudence would dictate that we also be well prepared for setbacks and unexpected challenges. And by doing so, we can, in fact, prevent these surprises from happening in the first place. For a country such as ours, with global interests, it is simply too dangerous to have a small force based on the assumption that world events will unfold only as we wish them to.

I am therefore proposing an enlargement of authorized personnel from the currently planned 1.36 million to 1.5 million. Of these additional forces, a full 100,000 will be in the combat units, increasing our total there by some 20 percent. This will give us the margin we need to ease the current strain of operations and to make more credible our commitments around the world.

New Initiatives

I want to describe for you the main changes that a prudent defense will make in our defense posture:

• We will strengthen and enlarge our ground combat forces, either forward deployed or more capable of rapid deployment, to the main areas of our interests in Europe, Asia, and the Middle East.

• We will retain Navy and Marine forces at current levels while emphasizing joint operations with ground forces where useful.

• We will be more selective in the use of U.S. troops for peace-keeping missions and more insistent on an international division of labor that speaks to the unique capabilities of those nations participating in such missions.

• We will reduce the Cold War size of the National Guard and redirect its efforts toward more combat service support and emergency preparedness rather than active combat duty. In addition, the National Guard will take the lead in homeland and civil defense, especially against weapons of mass destruction such as chemical and biological weapons.

• We will spend more on both procurement and research and development (R&D), especially those technologies that give us greater precision and control on the battlefield.

• We will increase efforts on ballistic missile defense and space defense.

• Finally, we will reduce our nuclear arsenal to levels established by the second Strategic Arms Reduction Talks (START II) when Russia ratifies that treaty, but we will not make unilateral reductions in the absence of such ratification.

To obtain such a prudent defense, I will propose to the Congress an increase in defense spending. The Congressional Budget Office estimates that the current defense budget falls short of funding our current force by some $11 billion per year. To fix that and carry out the proposals outlined here tonight, we will need to spend about $25 billion per year. I know some will say that we cannot afford to spend more on defense or that we should not spend more. The facts, however, are otherwise.

Currently the United States spends but 3.2 percent of its gross domestic product on defense, about 15 percent of the federal budget. This is the smallest amount of defense spending as a proportion of our national wealth and the federal budget since before Pearl Harbor. I propose to raise that spending slightly, to about 16 percent of future federal budgets. The issue therefore is not whether we can afford to spend more but rather whether we can take the risk of spending less. It is but a small premium to pay, especially when we are facing an era of possible budget surpluses.

The taxpayers of this nation, however, will never be satisfied with a plan that just adds resources. We know that defense can be run more efficiently. It is essential, therefore, that increased spending be accompanied by increased savings. Our plan calculates that another $5 billion per year can be saved if we pursue:

• Further base closings;

• Privatization of military maintenance and storage;

• More outsourcing of administration and logistics tasks to private firms;

• Reductions in management layers, especially in the Pentagon and other headquarters.

The time is also ripe for us to consider some other important changes. Should the Navy build new ships that fully exploit revolutionary new technologies or emphasize the upgrading of current weapons and ships? Should the Air Force invest so heavily in fighter aircraft or develop unmanned aircraft to operate over the battlefield as well as in space? Should the Army reorganize into more mobile and agile units or keep the large division structures that it has had for so very long? Should our reserve forces be assigned the primary mission of civil defense or emergency preparedness against terrorism in the United States?

I am directing the secretary of defense to create a special panel to study these and other matters so that our resources are most efficiently applied.

Speech One: A Prudent Defense

THE DECISION BEFORE US

My fellow Americans, I want to sum up the essence of the decision before us. Yesterday's clear and present danger has been replaced by today's spectrum of troubles and tomorrow's uncertainties. To protect our security, we must field a military force that can handle the major potential threats. It must also be capable of allowing us, in cooperation with our allies, to do the occasional peacekeeping mission.

We are still able to do that today. But will we be able to do so tomorrow? I have made the case tonight that our forces have been looking too much at peacekeeping and not enough at fighting wars; that we are spending too much on current operations and not enough on the future; that our troops are doing too much of the wrong thing and losing their edge. I have also argued that this can be remedied if we take prudent steps to fix the focus on the major potential threats; if we do less peacekeeping and, when we do it, share burdens more with our allies; if we redirect spending toward procurement and innovation; and if we increase the size of our forces and the size of the budget by 10 percent while pursuing strong cost-cutting measures. It may seem strange on the surface to offer a force that does less with more, but in order to correct our priorities, properly fund our forces, reduce the crippling strain on our troops, and invest in the future, it must be so.

Perhaps we should think of it this way. Our defense is an insurance policy. To keep that protection for the future, we need a little more insurance now even at the cost of a slightly higher premium.

Perhaps we should think of it in another way, too. As president, I can propose a plan, but without the support of you in Congress nothing will happen. Matters will drift until events—sometimes tragic events—dictate a change. We do not want to risk the hard-won gains of the past by lack of preparation for the future, the very risk we would run if our forces are unable to handle a major threat to the peace in Europe, Asia, or the Middle East. What is truly at stake in any defense policy is the legacy we leave for the next generation of Americans. We have the opportunity today to give our children and grandchildren a world safer than the one given us by our parents and grandparents. That is the most precious legacy we can leave for posterity. That is why we need a prudent defense.

SPEECH TWO: AN INNOVATIVE DEFENSE

A plan to take advantage of a time of relative peace and reduced threats by radically changing the U.S. military to capitalize on revolutionary technological advances and thereby be better prepared for the conflicts of the future—and within current spending levels

Members of Congress and My Fellow Americans:

I have decided to speak to you this evening because we have important decisions to make about our national defense. These decisions may very well affect the security of our nation for decades to come. As such, we will shape not only the security of our generation but that of our children and grandchildren.

As far as our security goes, we live now in a time of reduced threats—what our military experts call a strategic pause. The great triumph of the end of the Cold War has ushered in an unprecedented era of peace and cooperation among the major powers of the world. Market-based economic systems are the norm around the globe, and democracy is flourishing in more countries than ever before. There are still rogue regimes and organized violence and terrorism, to be sure, but these threats do not affect our basic security in the way that conflict among major powers might.

As we did during the years between World Wars I and II, we should use this time of strategic pause to experiment, innovate, and prepare our military for a very different future. During those interwar years, we experimented with aircraft carriers and naval aviation, tanks, amphibious warfare, high-speed fighter aircraft, and long-range bombers. We did this to be better prepared for future conflicts so that they would not have to be fought again in the style of the senseless stalemate that was the horror of World War I. Now too we must experiment with revolutionary new technologies not only to gain an advantage over our enemies but to deter war more effectively. We must not waste the peace dividend by keeping an overly large Cold War military force ready for action that is not likely to happen.

We have learned through hard experience that the secret of an effective defense is sound and timely preparation. We have also learned that in defense issues, no less than in our private lives, America's success has always come from our ability to innovate, not only through scientific discoveries but in their application.

And that is the challenge and decision before us. We are in the midst of what some have called a profound revolution in military affairs. Based on the advanced technologies of the information age, this revolution is as significant to the future of warfare as those technological advances that accompanied the industrial age in the last century. The weapons and ways of fighting wars that accompany this revolution in military affairs will change our strategy much as the tank, the radio, the airplane, the aircraft carrier, and the long-range rocket changed the nature of warfare in the past. And it promises to give us a far more effective military than we have ever had before. Those who master this revolution will be able to meet the threat and challenges of the future. Those who do not will be condemned to obsolescence. And that means defeat.

Fortunately we are living during a period of relative calm in world affairs and reduced danger to our vital interests. America is the sole superpower, and we are unlikely to be challenged by a major power in Europe or Asia for at least a decade. There are new threats, such as terrorism and international crime, that cannot be contained within borders. Other threats, such as rogue states or ethnic conflict, can be met by a broad coalition of forces including our allies and former adversaries. These threats, although diminished, should not be ignored. But because the immediate risks to our security are reduced, we have the opportunity—indeed the obligation—to redesign U.S. military forces that were designed 20 years ago to meet contingencies that, for the most part, faded with the collapse of Soviet power.

We must master the technological revolution and thereby prepare the United States to deal with the challenges of the future, a high-tech future in which military innovations can spell the difference between victory or defeat. The innovations I propose will make our military not only more effective against traditional threats but better prepared for the unconventional threats of the future. The innovative military force outlined here tonight can wage a campaign like that of Desert Storm with far fewer air, sea, and ground forces. Moreover, our future forces will be more prepared for adversaries who will not line up tanks in the desert but will use high-technology weapons such as sophisticated missiles and information warfare against American and allied forces. We can maintain our edge over these future challenges by recasting our forces now, while we have the time to do it.

The plan I propose tonight will achieve this objective.

1. It redirects our research and development priorities by emphasizing the new technologies.

2. It takes special measures to safeguard systems crucial to the warfare of the future so that the United States is not at risk of suffering a surprise technological strike that could cripple our information, communications, and computer networks.

3. It reshapes our forces to free up resources and to reflect the new ways of warfare.

I want to explain to you now just what threats we face, how the revolution in military affairs can deal with these threats, and the changes that we need to make.

Our defense planning begins with the definition of our interests and the threat to them. The lessons of the twentieth century have taught Americans that what we value most—our democratic freedoms—can be put at risk by events far from our shores. We have learned as well that our prosperity depends on a peaceful world. We have therefore made enormous sacrifices in lives and treasure to preserve our democracy and indeed to give democracy a fighting chance in the rest of the world. And in this we have succeeded. After two world wars, a third called the Cold War, and numerous other conflicts, the United States is secure and prosperous today.

This is still not a settled world, however, nor an entirely peaceful one. The headlines and television remind us that dangerous dictators are still at work, that states break up in civil or ethnic strife. We are working to incorporate former adversaries, such as Russia and China, into a more cooperative international system, but we do not know whether their experiments in political and economic reform will result in prosperous democracies. There is a danger, too, that weapons of mass destruction—nuclear, chemical, or biological—may be acquired by rogue states or terrorists.

Still, on balance, we are much less threatened today than we were only a few short years ago. The nuclear arsenals are being reduced. No major power in Europe or Asia will be able to challenge us militarily for some time. The rogue states, thanks to Desert Storm, know very well not to contest us in major warfare, although in the future we can expect them to probe for our weaknesses rather than pit themselves against our strengths as Iraq did in 1991.

Some would argue that this situation furnishes a basis for massive defense cuts or, at least, confidence in our long-term security. If we have any challenge, however, it is complacency. The hard-won efforts of previous generations have given us the precious gift of time, time to look ahead beyond the crisis of the moment, time to prepare for the military problems of the future.

War today wears many faces, from the sophisticated technician preparing the electronic guidance of advanced missiles to the fanatic in the streets armed with dime-store explosives. War in the future may be the silent action of weapons in space, the hum of computers selecting targets, and the surprise of a technological strike against satellites or computers when one side discovers itself blinded and unable either to locate the enemy or to communicate with its own forces.

In the future a military threat to the United States will most likely not be that of Desert Storm—where Saddam Hussein foolishly arrayed his large armored forces against us in an open desert. Future adversaries will seek to exploit their strengths against American weaknesses: They will attempt to cripple U.S. bases overseas by attacking them with chemical or biological weapons; they will prevent the long build-up of large American ground forces by hitting key supply areas and transportation hubs with cheap ballistic missiles like the Scud; they will attack our large aircraft carriers with inexpensive antiship cruise missiles and cheap sea mines; they will combat our multimillion-dollar aircraft with accurate ground-to-air missiles that cost only a few thousand dollars; and they will attempt to disrupt our communications and intelligence networks that rely so heavily on advanced automation and computerization. To combat these new tactics, the United States must create a technologically advanced force that is mobile, stealthy, and agile and that can attack targets from great distances. Such a force will not need huge forward bases or bulky supply lines, as it will be able to attack targets anywhere with a variety of sea-, space-, air-, or ground-based weapons. This is a very different force from the lethal yet ponderous military we have today.

When the Cold War ended, we possessed the world's most powerful military, with unmatched nuclear and conventional forces, a global reach, and advanced technology. The war in the Persian Gulf showed what we could do. Since then, we have reduced our military overall by one-third. I fully subscribe to that decision, which reflected both lesser threats and America's need to put its fiscal house in order. But that still leaves us with forces designed 20 years ago for a Cold War conflict that ended ten years ago. As a result, we are poorly prepared for the next wave of technological innovation that will successfully combat the threats of the future. Too much of our defense policy is mere tinkering with an increasingly obsolete structure that we cannot afford and do not need. Too much energy and investment is focused on being ready to fight two nearly simultaneous regional conflicts that are increasingly unlikely. By attempting to keep in readiness a military intended to meet the least likely event—a conventional war—we are courting instead a more likely disaster, a technological Pearl Harbor from a terrorist group or adversarial state using high technology or weapons of mass destruction to attack us where we are weak. That is because we are in the midst of a military-technical revolution that is available to everyone who seeks to take advantage of it.

I will try to define it for you.

THE MILITARY-TECHNICAL REVOLUTION

The first step to success on the battlefield is to know the adversary, to understand his capabilities or intentions, to know where he is, what he is doing, and the identity of his forces. The second step is to defeat the enemy through superior tactics, maneuver, and firepower. Until recently, all military efforts concentrated on creating ever greater masses of force and ever greater explosive power, the most spectacular example being the nuclear weapon. This required the mobilization of whole societies and, throughout the Cold War, the danger of nuclear holocaust.

But what if much of this is no longer necessary? What if we could locate the enemy precisely, strike him accurately from a long distance, and do so with a minimum of force? What if a network of sensors deployed on the ground, in the sea, in the air, and in space could pinpoint enemy movements with unerring accuracy? What then if computers could instantaneously process this information and relay it to a network of weapons that could launch and guide precision-munitions toward the enemy targets—with little danger to American forces who will no longer have to be engaged face-to-face with an enemy?

That is what the military-technical revolution is all about: the increasingly precise knowledge of the target's location and the increasingly accurate fire that can be brought against it from long range. The technological revolution that has given Americans unprecedented access to information can also give our defense forces unparalleled precision in finding and hitting the target.

This "what if" world is already with us. Let me give you a few examples:

- The World War I telegraph, the fastest transmitter of data in its day, sent 30 words a minute; this increased through Teletype to 66 words a minute by the early 1970s. Desert Storm computers, by comparison, processed 192,000 bits of information a minute. We can look forward to processing millions—even a trillion—bits of information as computer chips become more sophisticated. The trend is clearly toward even faster and smaller computers.

- During the Gulf War of 1991, one F-117 with laser-guided bombs destroyed the same type of targets that took 1,500 B-17 missions in World War II and 176 F-4 missions in Vietnam.

- Those same F-117 stealth fighters struck 40 percent of Iraq's strategic targets with only 2 percent of our total aircraft sorties.

- Tomahawk land-attack cruise missiles were able to find their marks with no risk to our forces.

- Also during the Gulf War, our space-based navigation satellites enabled allied forces to maneuver precisely across trackless desert.

I am saying, then, that new ways to locate the enemy precisely, to react rapidly, and to strike accurately are already transforming warfare as we know it. And this works both ways. The key to battle is not only the possession and use of this information but the denial of it to others.

And that is why I used the phrase "a technological Pearl Harbor." We are not the only ones exploring the frontiers of high technology. You must know, as I do, that the accuracy of even inexpensive missiles can already threaten $80 million aircraft. You must know, as I do, that systems already exist that would deny our forces some of the advantages that made the Gulf War such a massive success with so few casualties. An adversary need not build a huge and expensive military to challenge the United States today. An investment in weapons of mass destruction, ballistic missiles, and many high-technology weapons can be effective in denying American forces access to areas such as the Persian Gulf or the Straits of Taiwan. If our military forces are not prepared to combat these threats with information-age technology, they could suffer many casualties against a relatively small enemy.

The long, sad history of warfare gives many examples of how victorious nations became complacent with catastrophic results. In our own century, it was the victors of World War I who invented the tank, only to be crushed by the tank blitzkrieg of 1940. The German World War II tanks were not that much superior, but those who used them understood how they could revolutionize warfare. The victims had expected simply to fight the old way, even with new equipment.

The lessons are plain enough. We cannot prepare for yesterday's battles without risking the loss of tomorrow's wars. We cannot base our confidence solely on our ability to invent ever more sophisticated versions of the weapons used in those battles. We must use instead new weapons in new ways, with new organizations and new tactics, if we are to prevail next time.

I am therefore proposing the transformation of our defense through a revolutionary three-step program.

A THREE-STEP PROGRAM

1. Accelerate Research and Development (R&D) Spending to Reflect the New Priorities.

Our objective is to bring the new technologies of location, reaction, and accuracy on-line as fast as possible. I propose, therefore, that R&D spending rise over the next decade, instead of declining as currently planned. This will represent a $100 billion investment focused on emerging technologies such as:

- Weapon systems that can strike more precisely and at greater ranges;
- Increasingly smaller, more mobile computers and communications systems to make better and faster decisions and to maneuver more quickly;
- Information warfare technologies to cripple an adversary's command, control, communications, and computer facilities as well as protect our own;
- Stealth technologies and techniques to make all our forces harder to see and therefore less vulnerable to attack;
- Unmanned vehicles and robots to reduce the risk to our soldiers, sailors, airmen, and marines;
- New platforms for submerged power projection and undersea warfare;

• Space-based systems that not only support ground, sea, and air forces with better intelligence, communications, navigation, and weather forecasting but are also capable of delivering firepower anywhere in the world on a moment's notice.

2. Take Special Measures to Protect the Key Elements of the Military Revolution, Especially in the Area of Communications.
America's defenses will also be protected by a capability to deploy robust space-warfare capabilities and independent and integrated information-warfare capabilities. This will ensure that our nation never suffers a space or information strike like a crippling computer virus for which we are not prepared.

I also want to say a word here about missile defense. The United States cannot field today a ballistic missile defense system that would offer the protection we need at a cost we can afford. Clearly, however, our growing proficiency at finding and striking targets will lead us closer to our objective of eventually creating such a system. The technology is not yet ripe, and until it is we should concentrate our experiments around the most promising developments, such as the Navy's upper- and lower-tier programs, the Air Force's airborne or space-based laser systems, or the Army's theater missile defense experiments. Sometime in the future, small successes with these programs may enable us to build on them for an effective regional, then national, missile defense systems.

3. Reduce Our Planned Force Structure Over a Decade.
The purpose of this is both to free up resources and to create the new defense we need. We will gradually eliminate some Army divisions, tactical fighter wings, carrier battle groups, and the Air Force's older bombers and nuclear missiles. Systems and units that were originally fielded to fight the massive campaigns of the Cold War will be phased out. We will also reopen with Congress the issue of the size of the Marine Corps. The reorganization of our remaining forces into new units that fully exploit advanced technologies and new war-fighting concepts will more than offset their reduction in size.

As a result of these and other changes, the armed forces will be gradually reduced over the next decade to just under 1 million people versus the 1.45 million we have today. The reserve forces will also be cut by a commensurate amount. The reduction in this expensive force structure will free up the money we will need to revolutionize our military.

THE NEW U.S. MILITARY

Once the transformation of our forces is complete, the United States will field the most advanced and effective military in the world, truly up to the task of defending this nation's interests and objectives well into the 21st century. Instead of the current large, heavy forces designed to engage in direct and costly combat, we will emphasize long-range precision weapons and control of information to disrupt and defeat an adversary's ability to wage war.

For strategic missions, we will rely on a nuclear deterrent that will stay at levels established by the second Strategic Arms Reduction Talks (START II) until Russia ratifies that treaty and negotiations on further reductions bear fruit. These weapons of strategic warfare will be bolstered substantially by two other elements: first, our ability to carry out multidimensional long-range precision strikes; and second, our capacity to wage information warfare. Together, these will comprise a new strategic triad that replaces the old, purely nuclear arsenal. As our technological work progresses on the first two parts of this triad, we will gradually be able to reduce our nuclear weapons without any danger to the United States or without losing the effectiveness of our deterrent.

Our conventional forces will also be much changed. The Army and Marine Corps should include more than 30 information-intensive regiments and brigades. These smaller and more lethal units will also be mobile and stealthy in their own way. Some ground forces will be specifically focused on combat in cities and towns, since the world is increasingly becoming more urbanized. These forces will use robots and other advanced technologies to minimize casualties in urban operations. The Army's ground forces will be deployed principally by air and able to conduct decisive close-combat and land-based deep-strike operations anywhere in the world. Forward-deployed forces will be reduced, and marines will rely on smaller sea-based forces that emphasize stand-off weapons and unmanned aerial vehicles. This force will be capable of operating anywhere in the world without need of local bases.

Our Air Force will evolve into a Space and Air Force. Aircraft of the future will be stealthier, have more lethal weapons and longer ranges, and increasingly become unmanned—a move that decreases cost and could increase performance over piloted aircraft. Our Navy will begin to shift away from a carrier-based force to one that provides the same sort of mobile sea power through craft such as the arsenal ship, the stealth battleship, and the distributed capital ship. All these concepts use advances in information technology, stealth, and precision munitions to spread out increased naval firepower among many different and smaller ships. The large aircraft carrier, manned by over 5,000 sailors, is a magnificent vessel but is increasingly easy to find and vulnerable to cheap anti-ship missiles and torpedoes. I am afraid the day of the carrier will soon be over.

Finally, our reserve forces will operate unmanned aerial vehicles, micro robots, and satellites; pilot transport aircraft; and perform information warfare, network-management, and distributed logistics functions in direct support of our active forces. The reserves will also provide for the civil defense of the homeland and allow us to reinforce active forces in other combat and combat-support areas. The National Guard's heavy Cold War combat divisions will be eliminated, as I intend the innovation of our forces to apply to the total force, not just our active-duty units.

You cannot have a revolutionary change in our field forces without some similar change in the Pentagon itself. Our current organizational structure for national defense was created in 1947 and is over 50 years old. I have directed the secretary of defense to apply the same kind of innovative thinking to our defense bureaucracy as he plans for our fighting forces. Because technological innovation obscures the traditional boundaries between air, sea, and ground, perhaps we no longer need services organized along those traditional lines. In an era when a stealth submarine can effectively engage enemy tanks or an Army might have many assets based in space, does it make sense to separate the training of our services or still count our strength in ground divisions, air wings, and Navy carrier battle groups? In the digital age, when corporations are flattening hierarchies and sharing information across work groups, can the Pentagon not afford to trim its large and unwieldy organizational structure? Is our government, split as it is into various agencies with their separate responsibilities, even organized in the right way for information warfare? These are just some of the issues I would like to pursue with the same energy that we will use to remake our fighting units.

And here is some good news. We can acquire this revolutionary military force within the current defense budget of approximately $250 billion per year, using the reductions in force structure to give us the extra increments we need for both the new procurements and the additional R&D. By the end of the decade, however, we foresee a possible reduction of defense expenditures to the $220 billion range.

My fellow Americans, I realize that this plan contains its share of risks. Technological innovation is a gamble. There could be delays. A program of such magnitude usually takes more time and often more money than we expect. A smaller force will not be able to respond as robustly to situations such as that in Bosnia. Moreover, we are deliberately discarding forces that effectively deterred past threats, taking advantage of the current era of reduced danger to prepare for the future.

I am also aware that revolutions upset traditional structures and discard time-tested arrangements that have served us well. The real impediments to change are often more psychological than physical. We should not underestimate these difficulties, three of which deserve special attention.

1. The Cold War force structure will not go quietly into the night. We have managed to reduce our operating forces successfully since the early 1990s, only to discover that various peace-

keeping duties have imposed considerable strain. Yet while 130,000 sailors run the entire Atlantic Fleet, over 150,000 military and civilian personnel are assigned to the Washington, D.C., area to manage the military. I was astonished by that figure, and I know you are too. We are going to use a heavy hand to eliminate unnecessary layers of command and management.

2. The education of our military still reflects the older emphasis on hierarchies and separate services. We have taken great strides toward joint operations in recent years, but we still need greater emphasis from the outset on functional frameworks. Joint operations between our services should be the first, not the last, choice.

3. The United States and its allies are entering this revolution together. It is high time that we begin to plan as coalitions, not wait until a crisis forces us to look at a problem together. This means a much greater emphasis on training together ahead of events. Our allies, who for the most part have cut defense spending even more than we, are not launching into the military-technological revolution with the same enthusiasm we are. In order to keep systems compatible so that we can work together on the battlefield, I will redouble our efforts to bring our partners along in this endeavor.

As we work to overcome these problems, we can be sure of no end of controversy and a good deal of uncertainty. Some will argue that the risks are too great, others that the obstacles cannot be overcome. There will be honest differences of opinion over whether the technologies can work. I have already noted that our plans are based on a strategic estimate that rules out a large, Cold War–scale military problem for the better part of a decade, and some will see in this a serious error.

To those critics I say: Yes, we will still need some contingency capabilities; we will still be sending some old-fashioned forces to deal with some old-fashioned problems. And yes, American soldiers, marines, sailors, and airmen will still be going in harm's way. There is no avoiding the hard and brutal fact that war is about death. As one young officer said, "This modernization debate is only about budgets and bureaucratic turf if you don't have to go to war; for people who actually have to go to war, it's about living or dying."

We can do our best to deter; but deterrence may still fail, and we must still prevail. We will prevail because we will remain far superior to any potential adversary.

Ultimately, the defense of the United States is in the hands of those Americans who volunteer to defend us. I have a special message to those men and women of our armed services. The plan I put forward tonight may fill you with questions and lead you to doubt the future. Yet the purpose of this plan is in fact to secure the future. You who have studied war know better than I or your fellow citizens that the revolution in military affairs is not an option but a fast-dawning reality. You upon whom the burden falls to defend us with your lives know better than any other Americans the potential of this revolution and the peril in pretending we can avoid it. And it is because of my confidence in your capacity to make the changes successfully that I have decided upon such a revolutionary defense policy.

There is yet more to be said, this time to the American people. I have described several challenges to our national security tonight, chief among them, perhaps, a complacency about the future. I have said that the threat can be met by reordering our defense to accord with the new revolution so that we may field forces better able to find and strike the adversary, using the minimum power necessary to defeat him and providing the maximum protection of American lives in the process. I have also put forward a plan to pay for this reordering that balances the risks.

Yet we know our own history. Like many nations, we have been alerted to our deficiencies in defense only after suffering disaster. In the absence of a clear and present danger, it remains easier to drift along, secure in the memories of past triumphs. And this, and this alone, is in fact the clear and present danger.

I ask you tonight, therefore, to apply to our national security the same sense of alertness and adventure that distinguishes our civilian society. From the beginning of this republic, observers have been struck by America's eagerness to embrace change, our pride in revolutionary advances, our ability to remake our world even in the absence of any pressing need to do so. This is the high confidence that has made the United States the leader. And that is why I am so confident that with your support, we can embrace this military revolution and, by doing so, secure our future.

SPEECH THREE: A COOPERATIVE DEFENSE

*A plan to refocus our overly large and expensive Cold War
military on cooperative responses to the current challenges of
global security such as Bosnia and Haiti—and reduce overall
military spending by some 15 to 20 percent*

Members of Congress and My Fellow Americans:

Thank you for welcoming me to Capitol Hill this evening. I have
decided to speak directly to this special joint session of Congress
because we face important decisions that will affect our national
security far into the future. Since the end of the Cold War, we have
supported reduced but still very large armed forces. We have
hedged against threats and uncertainties not only to protect our
interests but also to shape the emerging international order. But
the world has changed; the risks have changed with it, and we need
to redesign our defense policy to accord with the new realities.

Despite being almost a decade on from the end of the Cold War,
we still find it difficult to shed the mind-sets, habits, vocabular-
ies, and policies born of nearly a century of unrelenting nation-
state confrontation. For much of this time, the fate of civilization
arguably hung in the balance. And yet today, we continue to
think in terms of us-versus-them outcomes rather than cooperative regimes of mutual security; of deterrence rather than assurance; of so-called rogue states rather than rogue leaders who hold
their populaces hostage; and of imagined or exaggerated threats
rather than diplomatic and economic initiatives designed to
improve long-standing relationships.

Let me be more specific. The dangers we face today come less
from a potential international rival, such as Russia or China, and
more from failing states, such as Somalia, Haiti, or Bosnia, which,
if allowed to fester, sooner or later will undermine the prospects

for general peace and prosperity. Other dangers come from non-state actors such as terrorists or international crime cartels. In addition, there are global problems such as environmental threats, changing demographics, refugees, and scarce resources that affect our security as much or more than an adversarial army. And the solution for such problems cannot only be "made in America" but must involve the international community of nations. The United States, as the preeminent power in the world today, must take the initiative to support such cooperative action because it is the most effective way to deal with these issues. In doing so, we will also be drawing together former adversaries and giving them an increased stake in international stability.

Such an approach requires an American military force and a defense strategy in accord with the new realities. I am therefore proposing a three-part plan:

1. We will reform U.S. forces to make them more effective in carrying out peacekeeping, small- and medium-scale interventions, and counterterrorism.

2. We will take the initiative to build up international institutions and alliances in a new cooperative effort that rallies America's allies and friends abroad to deal with these common problems. This effort will include leading the way in new arms control initiatives aimed at reducing nuclear arsenals and other weapons of mass destruction.

3. We will retain the capability for a swift military expansion in case of emergency while eliminating unnecessary forces and structure.

This plan will sharply reduce American defense expenditures and also strengthen our economy. But that is not the best reason to do it. The main purpose of our defense policy is, and must always be, to strengthen our security.

Our defense planning begins with the definition of our interests and the threat to them. The American people know that a secure and peaceful world is fundamental to our freedom and prosperity. America has forged important and growing trade links with

Europe, Asia, the Middle East, and our neighbors in the Americas. These links are part of the broadening definition of national security, which now places increasing emphasis on a robust economy rather than on the accumulation of arms. We have seen in the recent Asian financial crises how troubles in global markets can affect our security and prosperity.

Nonetheless, Americans should welcome this trend because it promises a world less afflicted by military competition. But such a world can come into being only when nations feel secure and stability is assured. There are more plowshares today than there used to be, yet there are still plenty of swords, and we also face a range of uncertainties that demands a strong defense.

NEW CHALLENGES

Since the end of the Cold War, our military strategists have been preoccupied with several problems, and I want to report on our progress.

First, reducing the nuclear threat. The end of the Cold War means that we need no longer fear a nuclear war that could end civilization. But huge arsenals still exist. Violent and irresponsible leaders might yet acquire weapons of mass destruction—nuclear, biological, or chemical—that can be used against the United States. We have therefore been working through arms control initiatives and sanctions against violators to reduce this danger. And, as you will hear tonight, I propose that we redouble our efforts in this most important task and take the lead in reducing nuclear arsenals even further.

Second, cooperating with former adversaries. Our former Russian adversaries are going through wrenching political and economic change. Working with NATO, the International Monetary Fund, and our own aid programs, we have attempted to foster a more cooperative and democratic Russia. Simultaneously, through NATO enlargement we have led the way toward securing the new democracies of Central Europe, and we have managed to do so while sustaining a cooperative relationship with Moscow.

These achievements have permitted reductions in U.S. forces deployed in Europe.

Turning to Asia, the policy of the United States is to foster constructive relations with the People's Republic of China, engaged in a profound transformation of the world's most populous nation. We have also worked with Japan and others to resolve conflicts; when necessary, we have reminded the region of our interest in free passage, free trade, and human rights. This policy, too, has allowed a smaller but still substantial American military presence.

Third, containing rogue leaders. American troops are most at risk today on the Korean peninsula, where a North Korean regime shaken by economic failure still threatens our South Korean ally with a huge military force. Nonetheless, we have made some headway in controlling North Korea's attempt to build nuclear weapons and in encouraging peace talks. Moreover, we have helped South Korea become a capable democratic ally, with armed forces that are more than a match for those of the North.

In the Persian Gulf, U.S. troops, ships, and aircraft are actively patrolling no-fly zones and helping to enforce sanctions against Iraq. The peace of the Gulf, however, is also endangered by Iran, a supporter of terrorism and a state also seeking nuclear and other weapons of mass destruction. Of late Iran has been making peaceful overtures to the United States that we hope will come to fruition. Nonetheless, we have been working with local allies and the United Nations to contain both Iraq and Iran, neither of whom has been able to harm our interests significantly since the Gulf War.

Fourth, stabilizing failed states. Revolutions in communications, the new global economy, the spread of ideas, and the end of ideologies are remaking the face of our world. We have seen huge movements of peoples—some as refugees, others as immigrants—all seeking a better life. But not every nation has been able to deal with these changes successfully. Some states have failed, disintegrating into savage civil wars. Old doctrines of racial and ethnic hatred have taken on new life through "ethnic cleansing" and other actions repugnant to our values. We have worked with the Unit-

ed Nations, NATO, and other avenues of international cooperation to stabilize such situations in places like Somalia, Haiti,
Bosnia, and Cambodia, with mixed success.

National security in the post–Cold War world is about much
more than guarding the Fulda Gap in Germany against an inva-
sion from the Warsaw Pact or deterring potential adversaries
with an overwhelming nuclear threat. Today, national security is
about economic relations with former allies and adversaries, the
human condition in the developing world, the mounting environmental challenges in industrial states, and stability in many different areas affected by the end of Cold War political structures.

As we have dealt with these issues, we have become more and
more aware of this fact: We need a broad and flexible military power,
but one very different than what we had before. Over the past several years, defense policy has been driven by the desire to reduce
the budget in line with the reduced threat and our domestic priorities, giving us a military smaller by one-third. But it is still a
force dominated by an obsolete nuclear and conventional structure, and it is still a force designed against the least likely threat—
a Soviet-style challenge. The result is to burden the United States
with a very expensive but misdirected military prepared for large-
scale warfare, while American forces are increasingly strained to
meet threats and carry out operations of a very different sort.

This cannot and should not continue. The essence of government is choice. Despite our great power, the United States cannot meet every contingency. The vain attempt to do so only
stretches our resources and gives us inadequate forces at the same
time. Instead, we must hedge against uncertainties yet retain
enough capability for rapid response in the case of a clear and present danger.

An effective defense policy for our times, therefore, begins
with a choice. Which threats are receding, soon to be part of the
history books? Which challenges are approaching, for which we
should prepare ourselves? What do we hedge against, and how do
we do it?

As the Cold War era fades from our memories, the answers to
these questions have become clearer:

- Today and for the foreseeable future, the Soviet-style threat is gone. There are no global rivals to the United States, and there will be none for a decade and probably longer.

- Today and for the foreseeable future, the threat from the so-called rogue states is decreasing. Iraq is crippled. North Korea is failing. These states cannot expect aid from a superpower; their economies are disasters; and their regimes must change, for it is not the people of Iraq and North Korea who are a threat but their incompetent rulers. Their militaries were no match for America's capabilities in the past, as we demonstrated in Desert Storm. We are even further ahead of them now, and the gap is widening.

- Today and for the foreseeable future, the nuclear threat, aside from the danger of terrorism and proliferation, is substantially diminished. The issue is not whether the reduction in nuclear arsenals will continue but rather how quickly the major powers can reduce them. Even the dangers of proliferation or terrorism are on a much different scale from the nuclear standoff of yesteryear. We will diminish this threat even more by leading the effort to disarm even further.

The real challenges are of a different order. The problems of failed states, civil wars, and refugees originate within borders but become most dangerous when they cross borders or even dissolve them. You know some of the names: Somalia. Haiti. Rwanda. Bosnia. Cambodia. No region has been spared.

We must not underestimate the impact of this problem. Like a spreading virus, the ideologies, passions, and refugees let loose by such failed states can infect a region. And while we and our allies might like to ignore or downplay the matter, the cumulative impact of our inaction will eventually undermine our own safety. Crimes are being committed, and criminals take note of our reaction.

Let us be honest with ourselves. We have had a very mixed record thus far in dealing with such crises partly because we were unprepared for them. Peacekeeping and stability operations are not what America planned to do when we designed our armed forces during the Cold War. Our soldiers, sailors, marines, and airmen are trained to fight wars, not win the peace. They train to find the enemy, seize the strategic ground, advance, and defeat the adversary. Peacekeeping is not like that, not like that at all.

The training problem presents its own challenge to our military professionalism, but the United States also faces a special dilemma in dealing with peacekeeping operations.

The dilemma is this: American involvement, especially with our troops, may go beyond our immediate interests. We cannot be the policeman of the world, summoned whenever anything goes wrong anywhere. But American refusal to become involved often signals the absence of action by other members of the international community. This may eventually create a threat to our interests when a situation spirals out of control. We cannot simply abdicate our leadership when it comes to international order.

There is only one way to police the world without America becoming the policeman. That is to have effective U.S. military forces acting primarily in conjunction with other nations and international institutions so that burdens and risks are shared and every crisis does not become primarily an American responsibility. To do this, we will increasingly rely on diplomacy and preventive actions to resolve conflicts before they happen and to work through multilateral approaches to solve them when they occur.

A THREE-POINT PROGRAM

That is why I am proposing tonight a three-point program that reshapes our forces to deal with both the decreased need for large deterrent forces and the increased need for a multilateral effort that assures international stability. The strategy outlined by this plan will transform our military into an institution uniquely suited to deal with the new problems of the post–Cold War world and at the same time leave us with an effective residual capability for conventional military action.

Speech Three: A Cooperative Defense

1. Rebalance Our Forces to Meet Today's Spectrum of Threats.
We will gear a larger proportion of our military toward the conduct of effective counterterrorism operations, small- and medium-scale intervention, and peacekeeping or stability operations. We should equip such forces with the latest technology for their missions, taking advantage of both the air power and information revolutions. And we must ensure that they can be deployed swiftly.

We will also strengthen our military capabilities—both conventional and special—particularly those designed to improve cooperation with the militaries of other nations. These capabilities include the following:

- An emphasis on long-range precision munitions that will reduce danger to our close-combat units and that will make coalition and alliance forces more effective;

- Recognition of the importance of information warfare, including surveillance and reconnaissance systems, and improved communications;

- A greater role for increased numbers of special operations units able to act in conjunction with those of our allies;

- Greater emphasis on combat support and service support. Again, this is an area where we can offer a unique strength that multiplies the effectiveness of allied forces but does not substitute American power for allied efforts.

2. Create More Effective International Security Mechanisms.
Much of American foreign policy has been designed to establish effective international organizations that transform national competition into cooperative action. Through NATO in Europe and the U.S.-Japan security treaty in Asia, we have created communities of common interest where in fact these rules are followed. As we have seen, however, the international community still lacks a practical security design that would combine diplomatic efforts with an effective international military force.

The United States alone, as I have said earlier, cannot and should not become the world's policeman. That leaves two choices in dealing with the failed states and potential aggressors of the post–Cold

War world: the United Nations or regional allies. Our initial post–Cold War effort to vest military responsibilities in the United Nations may have been premature, but it was not wrong. The wise men who established the Security Council in 1945 foresaw the necessity for the international organization to have forces at its disposal. No less a figure than Winston Churchill, in the forgotten part of his "Iron Curtain" speech, repeated his support for such a U.N. force that would draw upon dedicated national units. I will therefore suggest to the Security Council and the secretary general that this subject be put again on the agenda. There need not be a permanent standing force under the control of the United Nations, but the organization should definitely have more reliable access to international forces in a crisis. In this way, we might be able to avoid disasters like that in Rwanda in 1994, when the massacres continued while the United Nations scrambled to find forces for a peacekeeping mission.

The United Nations, however, is not the only approach to the problem. America is blessed with strong allies and numerous friends. Together, we have common interests in stabilizing the international order. Some of our allies also have powerful if limited military forces, and others are prepared to offer economic assistance. We already have experience with allied cooperation in Bosnia through both the NATO command and the European rapid-reaction force. We have also benefited from the cooperation of other states, including Russia, Poland, Hungary, the Czech Republic, and others. In Africa, a low-cost experiment in training a regional crisis response force has been surprisingly successful.

The time has come, therefore, to make these arrangements more permanent. Our initial proposal will be to establish permanent rapid-reaction units drawn from a coalition of those powers able and willing to cooperate. In these units, as in the overall planning, there should be a division of labor, each party doing what it does best. Militarily, this will mean in most cases the deployment of unique American assets, such as logistics and airlift, rather than major American combat units, although we should be prepared to deploy the latter in case of emergency. This was what was done in Somalia on an ad hoc basis, as the United States led 26 other nations in an improvised coalition to relieve the horrible famine there. The key to success now is to find the degree to which we can institutionalize that sort of spontaneous reaction.

Too often in the past, American defense planning has been conducted in a vacuum, without fully recognizing the like-minded states that become our partners in almost any military operation. Today, the question is not whether a mission will be unilateral or multilateral—it is a question of what kind of multilateral operation we will choose to do. I am convinced that we do not take full advantage of our long-term alliances and our short-term partners who have similar interests in many different security concerns. We must integrate more fully the efforts of our allies into this new cooperative scheme. This will include encouraging allies to maintain vigorous defenses, as many have slashed their defense budgets or disarmed too soon. For our part, we must also let allies lead in the smaller missions of collective security, especially when they have greater interests at stake. The United States need not lead everywhere and in every cause to maintain its superpower status.

3. Restructure Our Forces to Reflect Our New Strategic Situation and Priorities.

This means the overdue retirement of a Cold War structure that is wasteful and not up to the job. Over the next seven to ten years, we will therefore retire 30 percent of the current active force. This smaller military will rely heavily on the reserves in case of emergency. The new defense policy places greater emphasis on reserve air power, combat support, and combat service support functions—all areas in which reserve component forces have excelled. Resources will be redirected to ensure the National Guard can deploy five fully ready brigades within 90 days of a mobilization. These moves do not come without cost, and I will tell you tonight that our military will be less able to respond to large challenges as quickly as it has in the past. However, this is a risk that is low and well worth taking. It is simply a waste of money and other resources to keep a huge military force on hair-trigger readiness in the post–Cold War world.

A critical part of our plan will also be to hedge against further threats. New technologies and systems will be developed and tested as prototypes but need not be manufactured in quantity unless the threat should warrant it. As part of this approach, I favor research into ballistic missile defenses as a hedge, but no deployment will be necessary any time soon. We will certainly not take any action that might jeopardize the Anti-Ballistic Missile (ABM) Treaty we have adhered to for the past 26 years.

Clearly, this much smaller and more suitable force carries with it dramatic changes in the military budget. Active-duty forces will be reduced from the current 1.45 million people to less than 900,000. There will be just over 700,000 personnel in reserves. Our nuclear forces will be reduced considerably. All in all, we will be trimming our military costs from 3.2 percent of gross domestic product and 15 percent of the federal budget to about 2 percent and 9.4 percent, respectively, over a five-year period. If all our efficiency measures are realized, these costs will translate into annual defense expenditures of about $205 billion a year after 2003, substantially below the current level of $250 billion. But the procurement part of the budget will go up after 2003 to an average of $47 billion from the current $44 billion, and research and development will increase as well.

This new force will raise important issues of military organization and tactics. I have therefore asked the secretary of defense to investigate these questions:

- How can we combine our own and allied research into ballistic missile defense to advance the common cause?

- Can the current unit structures of the Army and Marine Corps be changed to give us similar effectiveness with less personnel?

- How can we change the current industrial base to accord with the prototype approach that demands quality research and experimentation but not an expensive procurement?

- How can we create specialized units in both the active force and reserve for peacekeeping and humanitarian relief operations?

- How can we retrain much of the reserve forces and some active forces to specialize in homeland defense, especially information warfare, counterterrorism, and protection against weapons of mass destruction used against the United States itself?

Let no one think that these changes will leave us with a weak military. At the end of it all, we will have a conventional force some 30 percent smaller across the board but more than adequate for the types of challenges we will face in today's world. We will continue to keep forces forward deployed in both Asia and Europe, but in reduced numbers and at a reduced cost. If we had to fight a major conflict in either of these theaters, which I do not expect will happen, we will reinforce our small forward-deployed forces with active and reserve forces mobilized and sent from the United States. Money saved from closing bases both overseas and in the United States will be used to increase the amount of strategic airlift we have, replacing large forward-based troops with more mobile units that can be flown to crisis areas with little notice.

Our expensive and largely redundant nuclear force will be reduced to Strategic Arms Reduction Talks (START) III levels, pending negotiations with the Russians on further reductions. I am convinced, however, that we can safely afford to reduce much further, and I have asked the National Security Council to explore other initiatives such as de-alerting most of our nuclear force while asking the other nuclear powers to follow suit. One of the most striking failures of our current nuclear debate is that we have come to regard 2,000 nuclear warheads as a small number. In fact, it is a large and expensive-to-maintain number that makes no political or military sense. In this day and age, we must question past concepts of deterrence that predicate themselves on a large nuclear arsenal. That is the sort of old thinking we can now safely challenge—a challenge for which we will reap many rewards.

My fellow Americans, I can think of few periods in our history when greater changes were demanded of our armed forces than those I am proposing. Some will see in this program a dangerous disarmament. They are wrong. In fact, the "cooperative defense" I have discussed with you is a program for *arming* America with the forces we need to meet the challenges of the new era. The United States will possess the most powerful standing military on earth by a substantial margin. We will certainly be able to defend the United States, its territories overseas, and the areas that are vital to our national interest. We will also be more able to respond to those challenges that are most important in the post–Cold War world.

Today's threat, I repeat, is not the sudden reappearance of a Soviet-style attack. It is not the break-out of a rogue regime. It is not a superpower nuclear arms race. These are dangers largely in the past. By keeping too large and outdated a military against such receding dangers, we only weaken ourselves in dealing with the real problems, whether they are national competitiveness or failed states. And instead of meeting those challenges, we are wasting untold sums on the wrong forces for the wrong occasions. It is a mistake to believe that the spending of money alone will guarantee our safety. There is no such thing as deterrence by appropriation.

The United States must therefore re-equip, retrain, and reorganize our forces to deal with the real issues. We must also revive and redouble our efforts to recruit international cooperation to deal with security problems of common interest. There are trade-offs, naturally. The United States will no longer be able unilaterally to send large military forces to several crises at once and will depend greatly on preventive diplomacy and allied support to assist in those instances. In the unlikely event of a significant conflict, it will take time to mobilize the National Guard and Reserve in order to reinforce our smaller active forces. These are risks, however, that are well worth taking. I am confident that with your support, the Americans who volunteer to protect us all through military service will master these new challenges with the same "can do" enthusiasm we have come to expect.

There is a good military term that sums up the idea behind a cooperative defense. It is called a "force multiplier." Our armed services, combined with those of our allies abroad, using international mechanisms, will multiply the effort to secure the blessings of peace and freedom. The methods will be different from those of the past, but the result will be the same: a safer future for America and, through cooperation in the common interest, for the rest of the world as well.

SPEECH FOUR: A BALANCED DEFENSE

*A plan to keep a slightly smaller military focused on
near-term challenges and prepared to meet many different
threats, ranging from deterring rogue states to peacekeeping
in failed states—and at constant spending levels*

Members of Congress and My Fellow Americans:

Thank you for welcoming me to Capitol Hill this evening. It has
long been customary for presidents to address Congress directly
in times of emergency or to advocate change. But I have decided to speak to you tonight for a different reason. I am asking you
to support continuity, to stay the course in American defense
policy. The reason is simple: Only by pursuing our current course
can we defend American security in the most balanced way.

In the wake of the Cold War, aggression by a single powerful
adversary no longer threatens the United States. Nonetheless, we
still face a series of dangerous uncertainties stretching out into the
next century. The United States and its allies could be menaced
by an act of terrorism, the attack of a rogue state, or, over the longer
term, the appearance of a major rival. You also know that our forces
have been deeply engaged in peacekeeping missions to secure order
and hope in countries affected by civil war and collapsed govern-
ments. We therefore need a flexible balance of forces to deal with
these contingencies, forces that rely upon a realistic assessment of
the threats and that apportion our resources carefully between current operations and future needs. And this is what we have done
despite a military one-third smaller than at the end of the Cold
War.

But now some want to change the course.

You may have heard or read that our military is too small, or
that we are spending too little, or that we are overextended in peace-

keeping. Others argue that we are missing a technological revolution that will leave us with an obsolete defense. And still others claim that we are spending way too much and can reduce our defense effort by another 30 percent.

All of these ideas are mistaken because they pay too much attention to a single problem at the cost of neglecting the others. Those who would spend more money focus upon the receding dangers of major attacks in Europe or Asia while ignoring America's necessary role in keeping the peace. The technological revolutionaries would risk our defense on weapons, organizations, and tactics that are best approached on a gradual "prove as you go" fashion. Finally, we would risk our credibility abroad, and invite a hostile challenge, if we made huge further reductions in our forces without a commensurate reduction in the threats.

We are not going to make these mistakes. We are not going to increase spending on the wrong forces, and we are not going to abandon necessary peacekeeping missions. We are not going to risk our security with a roll of the technological dice. And we are certainly not going to jeopardize our international leadership and our vital interests by a dangerous reduction in the size of our armed forces.

STAYING THE COURSE

Instead, we are going to stay the course with a balanced defense. Naturally, I am not promising you the moon at little or no cost. There are trade-offs that I shall explain later. The balanced approach I propose, however, provides for an efficient defense and gives us the flexibility to adjust our course when necessary. Part of my purpose in speaking to you is also to outline a few of those adjustments that will continue to give us the forces we need. These include:

1. Greater emphasis on proven technological and organizational innovation that will allow slightly smaller forces to be more effective;

2. Increased procurement for new and replacement equipment to prepare for the future;

3. More effective spending of our resources.

The achievement of these objectives is the best investment we can make for our future.

Let me begin with the most basic issue in planning our defense: our interests and the threats to those interests. The lessons of the twentieth century have taught Americans that what we value most—our democratic freedoms—can be put at risk by events far from our shores. And these events can also threaten our prosperity. Today, we have trading relationships with Europe, the Middle East, and Asia that are vital to the health of the American economy. Since 1970, the percentage of our gross national product derived from international trade has tripled and is rising. As we have seen from the recent Asian economic crises, instability in one area of the world can easily affect our economic health. Our military should be regarded not only as the defenders of our democracy but also as the shield of our prosperity.

The sacrifices made by this and previous generations in defense of the United States have paid off. Today our democracy is secure. We are at peace, and we are prosperous. But we would be rash indeed if we took this for granted, thereby putting at risk the legacy for our children and our grandchildren.

Unfortunately, the end of the Cold War did not mean the end of trouble in the world, either for others or for ourselves. Let me discuss briefly a few of the problems we face abroad that could menace our interests.

1. *Dangerous rogue states.* North Korea is on the brink of starvation and without allies. Yet this same country remains armed to the teeth, its troops poised to invade South Korea. In the Persian Gulf, Iraq still possesses enough military power to threaten its neighbors in the absence of U.S. air, sea, and land power. Iran, a supporter of terrorism, seeks nuclear and other weapons of mass destruction. To protect our interests and our allies, we must therefore have forces capable of deterring aggression

simultaneously in both Asia and the Middle East. In 1998, however, we can accomplish this mission with less force than in the recent past.

2. *Collapsing nations.* The end of the twentieth century is a time of great change. We live in a revolutionary era when the international economy and global communications have raised expectations around the world. But not every nation and not every state has been able to deal successfully with such changes. Some states have buckled and broken down into savage civil wars. Bewildered peoples, frightened by demagogues, have sought safety once more in the doctrines of racial hatred and ethnic cleansing that we hoped had been consigned to history. These threats to international order challenge our fundamental values and sometimes our national interests, for the spread of such doctrines would negate everything we have worked so hard to achieve. We must therefore be able to act militarily where necessary, in cooperation with other nations, to restore peace, order, and hope.

3. *The nuclear threat and weapons of mass destruction.* The end of the Cold War means that we need no longer fear a nuclear war that could end civilization. But huge arsenals still exist, and violent and irresponsible leaders might yet acquire nuclear weapons. Worse still, we may yet see chemical or biological weapons in the wrong hands, mounted on missiles capable of reaching the United States. Those who might be tempted to challenge us in this way must know that American retaliation would be swift, sure, and devastating. The danger is especially acute when it comes from terrorists, who increasingly will have access to these weapons.

4. *Potential rivals in Europe or Asia.* We are free today of a major international rival. Russia is going through wrenching political and economic change. In Asia, the policy of the United States is to foster constructive relations with the People's Republic of China, the world's most populous nation, also engaged in a profound transformation. But the outcome of these unprecedented experiments is uncertain, and we cannot fore-

cast how they will end. In the meantime, NATO, Japan, and our other friends and allies must rely upon the presence of American forces to sustain secure and cooperative relationships. Indeed, the very commitment of those forces supports our diplomacy as we expand NATO to increase security in Europe, and as we encourage both Russia and China to join an international community they opposed until very recently. Forward-deployed American forces, albeit in smaller numbers, are therefore still essential to the overall security of Europe and Asia.

CHANGES WE HAVE MADE

Since the end of the Cold War, we have been very much aware of these contingencies, and we have rebalanced and reshaped the Cold War–era military to deal with them. We have retained our basic strategy: To secure our interests, we must be able to deter and to defeat challenges to our security in Europe, Asia, and the Middle East. And we have retained a basic benchmark for our military capabilities: We must be able to deal with crises in more than one region simultaneously. At the same time, we have recognized that the potential challenges have diminished so that we have been able to achieve our objectives with smaller forces and at much less cost.

If, for instance, we were to respond again to aggression from Saddam Hussein, we could do so with much less force than in 1991. While we have decreased our forces by over one-third since the Gulf War, during the battles of Desert Storm we reduced the military might of the Iraqi Army and Air Force by an even greater percentage. Similarly a less-threatening situation prevails in Korea, where the forces of our ally South Korea greatly outclass those of the rogue regime in the impoverished North.

I recognize that it may appear unrealistic to expect smaller American forces to fight and win in two major regional conflicts simultaneously. It may also seem unrealistic to expect two such conflicts to happen at once. Our strategy therefore will indeed center on being able to respond effectively to nearly simultaneous crises around the globe but not on an attempt to fight two Desert Storms at the same time. Instead, through the use of airpower and in conjunction with our regional allies, we will deter or halt aggression until we can mobilize the ground forces needed to win a decisive victory in any theater. This military, which is also prepared for peacekeeping and other operations in places such as Bosnia, is an effective, albeit smaller force for a more efficient American strategy.

Many Americans do not realize the enormous changes that have already taken place, especially our effort to reduce unnecessary defense expenditures. Let me give you a few figures:

- In 1985, at the height of the Cold War, we spent the 1997 equivalent of almost $400 billion on defense; today we spend around $250 billion per year.

- In 1989 Defense took 28 percent of the federal budget; today it takes 15 percent.

- In 1989 Defense took 7 percent of our gross national product; today it takes 3.2 percent.

Reductions in active-duty personnel have been even more significant, from 2.2 million in 1989 to 1.36 million by the end of 1999. Two hundred thousand U.S. troops are deployed overseas now, compared with 500,000 then. Our defense industry has also been transformed. Instead of 3.7 million workers and a $120 billion yearly procurement budget, today the defense effort employs 2.2 million workers, and the procurement cost is $44 billion.

I do not regret these reductions, for there is nothing that hurts both our security and our economic health more than a huge, unnecessary waste of resources. Americans should also applaud the way our forces have adapted to their new conditions. Our soldiers, sailors, marines, and airmen have retained their readiness, their spirit, and their "can do" attitude despite increased deployments and decreased budgets. Today's armed services consist of highly trained professionals, capable of dominating the battle on land, sea, and in the air. We are the leaders in using space for communications, navigation, intelligence, and many other functions. And we have preeminent nuclear forces.

Now the time has come for a further rearrangement of our defense to give it the balance we need for the future. Let me draw upon a common experience. We know that if the tires on our cars are just slightly out of line, the tire itself will eventually be ruined. Today, our defense posture is slightly out of line. By correcting it now, we will spare ourselves a lot of damage later.

As we reduced the size of the military and reshaped it, we hedged against the uncertainties of the post–Cold War era by emphasizing readiness and operations over research, investment, and procurement.

These proportions must now be altered so that our forces will be adequately equipped for the future.

A FOUR-POINT PLAN

I am happy to report that we can make these changes within the current budget of approximately $250 billion. And we can do it without upsetting the careful balance of forces that allows us to deal with the full range of potential threats.

I am therefore proposing a four-point plan for a more balanced defense. This plan will sustain our ability to deal with simultaneous challenges to American interests in more than one region while preparing our forces for the threats of the future through new emphasis on research, investment, and procurement.

1. *We will carefully pursue technological innovation that increases our ability to find the enemy and strike him with great accuracy.* Although I have warned against a full-fledged commitment to revolutionary new technologies that are largely unproven, we must increase our emphasis on tried-and-true technological advances, especially capabilities in communications, intelligence, and space. We will need to protect our military and commercial satellites from attack or disruption by an adversary. High-tech forces that wage war from a greater distance require

more targeting data, precise navigational information, and the rapid distribution of information. Advances in these fields can also facilitate timely identification of missile launches, a key element in our continuing program to research missile defenses.

2. *We will increase our procurement where warranted as we reshape the forces.* Procurement of new equipment has been too low for too long. We will raise procurement levels from the current $44 billion to nearly $55 billion over the next several years. This does not mean, however, that we will buy unnecessary weapons. For example, our warplanes and warships so outclass the competition that we do not need to procure large numbers of newer systems beyond those currently planned. Technological advances will also enable us to reduce the size of active-duty forces while still retaining much of their firepower. This means smaller units in all the services that can do more with less manpower.

3. *We will conduct defense more efficiently.* To do what we need to do without increasing the overall budget means we must tackle long-overdue reforms. One is to close more surplus bases. Just look at the numbers. Force structures and manpower are down 33 percent since the end of the Cold War, but base structures are down only 25 percent and in the United States only 20 percent. Dealing forthrightly with this issue can save at least $3 billion a year for the taxpayers. I know that this is a tough issue for the Congress, but it is an even tougher issue to deny our troops what they need as a consequence. To save even more, we will privatize more of the Pentagon's spending. The Defense Science Board estimates that $10 billion could be saved this way. It is worth the effort, even if the savings turn out to be less.

4. *Lastly, we must change the way in which we rotate and deploy our troops.* As you may know from many recent reports, the repeated deployments of our military have strained the force. I am convinced that we need not have either a larger force or a more expensive one. But to alleviate this damaging strain on our people and our equipment, we must manage the force that we do have with greater efficiency. A new system of rotat-

ing overseas deployments will let a slightly smaller force undertake all of today's security challenges without a negative impact on readiness or morale.

All told, changes in force structure and organization will allow us to reduce the U.S. military from the current 1.45 million active-duty troops to about 1.3 million. The reserve forces will be cut from 900,000 to 700,000 troops.

These measures can save the Department of Defense up to $15 billion per year. Some of that money is needed to make up for the current underfunding of the Pentagon's budget. The rest will go to fund the procurement of new and replacement weapon systems, although I have proposed cutting back on the planned purchases of certain tactical aircraft, submarines, and ships.

This program for a more balanced defense avoids serious errors that could badly damage our military and with it our national security over the long haul.

Some people think that more defense spending means more security. They are wrong. Keeping a force structure larger than the one we need actually weakens our defense for the long term while diverting resources from necessary investments, whether in procurement, training, or research. We do not face today a fundamental security threat from Russia, China, or elsewhere, and we do not need to build up an additional force structure to deal with a potential rival a decade or more away.

Others, alarmed by the complexities of peacekeeping, argue that we should abandon this necessary mission. The critics of our peacekeeping missions offer a seductive argument: Would we not be better off simply concentrating on deterring rogue states, reducing the residual nuclear threat, and sustaining our alliances in Asia and Europe? Why cannot others, our allies, or the United Nations, do the peacekeeping job?

My answer to this is "yes," we most definitely should call upon our allies and friends, and even the United Nations, to help. But you know, as I do, that when all is said and done, that will not be enough to protect our interests, advance our values, or defend our security.

Speech Four: A Balanced Defense

The post–Cold War world and our hopes for a better international order are being put to the test by collapsing states, civil strife, ethnic hatreds, and all the situations that have required peacekeeping. This is not simply a humanitarian issue, although that would be a very strong reason to act. We must think of the impact of cumulative inaction upon our strategy of deterring aggression. We avert our eyes from this peacekeeping obligation only at greater peril. Surely the lesson of the twentieth century is that those with evil in their hearts see the failings of good men and women in lesser crises as a sign of deeper and more dangerous flaws.

Make no mistake. Having won the Cold War, we are being summoned now to win the peace. The prospects for that peace depend upon the United States. Our wisdom, our will, our wealth, and our muscle will go far to determine the character of the new century. If we do not lead, then no one else will do so. If we are unwilling to tackle the peacekeeping mission, then the peace will not be kept.

There are those, too, who criticize a balanced defense because they are caught in the spell of seductive new technologies. Americans have always been fascinated by such developments. We pioneered the modern age through invention and ingenuity. Give us a problem, we say, and we will fix it with a machine. Very often we do. But not always.

Defense is a hard, exacting task. There are many disappointments along the way. Matters do not always work out as planned. What we must avoid at all costs is reliance on what the soldiers call the "silver bullet"—the idea that some technological magic will just fix it all around. We went down that road a decade ago with what some term "Star Wars," the quest for a missile defense. I hope some day we can deploy one that works. But so far we have not found it, and we cannot plan our security around one.

You know from your own experience that everything works fine, and then the computer goes down. Sometimes it is not so easy to bring it back up.

I am therefore proceeding carefully with what some have called a "revolution" in military affairs. We are going to adapt our forces as need be, but we are not going to gamble the future of our security on unproven technologies, no matter now exciting they appear to be.

Finally, we must not accept the views of those who play down the dangers we face and would, in the name of economy, make major reductions in the military. There is simply no way for the United States to be prepared to meet rogue state threats in Asia and the Middle East, to keep forces deployed in Europe, or to carry out peacekeeping missions with a force smaller than the one I propose. Just consider the risk to our interests. If confronted by a crisis in more than one region, we would have to make an agonizing choice: What is most important, our security in Asia, in Europe, or in the Middle East? The American people would never forgive a president for such a lack of foresight or preparation. A safer rule is this: Do not reduce the forces unless the risks are reduced beforehand. I have weighed the risks carefully and consider this force the minimum needed to undertake all the strategic tasks that support our foreign policy. This smaller force has limits, but they are well within the acceptable range of risks for our strategy.

The changes I propose will not give us a larger force than we field today but one that is formidable and effective. The nuclear deterrent will remain largely the same, although after Russia ratifies the second Strategic Arms Reduction Talks (START II), the United States will lead the push for the ratification of START III. In this day and age, there is no need to keep an expensive and overly large nuclear deterrent when a smaller and more efficient nuclear force will have the same overall effect. The United States will also lead the way in nonproliferation efforts as well as arms control agreements in further efforts to reduce the nuclear powers' dependence on large arsenals.

Because the entire active force will drop from 1.45 million personnel to 1.3 million by 2003, the Army and Air Force will lose some troops, but they will keep their combat power. Changes in technology, organization, and doctrine will allow smaller units to wield the same lethality on the battlefield as did the larger units of the past. The Navy will retain a 12-carrier force, which is needed to extend our global presence and fighting power. The United States will also retain its forward deployments in Europe,

Asia, and the Persian Gulf, although they will be reduced in size by some 10 to 15 percent. Smaller reserve forces will be focused on homeland defense and providing support to active-duty troops during overseas deployments. We will increase spending on new weapons, research and development, and continue to experiment with, but not deploy, projects such as a national missile defense.

In the meantime I have asked the secretary of defense to explore several concepts that will further tailor our military to the challenges of the future. These include:

- How can the Pentagon take advantage of changing business practices to streamline its administrative procedures and organizational structure?

- How can our troops best train to be equally proficient at both peacekeeping and combat operations?

- Should we prepare military units specifically for peacekeeping duties?

- How can new readiness and rotational policies be implemented to alleviate some of the strain on frequently deployed units?

- How can the United States reduce its overseas presence without upsetting the balance of power in a particular region or America's leadership role in her alliances?

The answers to these questions will help us continue to provide an efficient defense without a future increase in the Pentagon's budget.

STEADY AS WE GO

Members of Congress, the balanced defense plan I have put before you prepares us for the potential dangers ahead. It avoids the serious blunder of abandoning the peacekeeping responsibility. And it brings a sharper focus to the overall defense plan by shifting the emphasis from large and expensive combat forces kept at hair-trigger readiness to research and procurement for the future. We are not going to make the mistake either of spending too much where we are already strong enough, risking too much on emerging technologies, or abandoning essential missions. The current defense budget will not increase, but neither will it decrease.

As we look forward, the motto "steady as we go" is the most efficient choice in defense policy. In the past, more often than not, the United States has pursued a different and less wise course, that of arming suddenly to meet a crisis and then disarming quickly once the crisis has passed. This is a wasteful and costly way to run our national defense. It deprives our peacetime diplomacy of leverage and invites trouble from our adversaries. We simply cannot afford to do business that way any longer.

Since the end of the Cold War, we have sought to avoid such a "feast or famine" defense policy. The uncertainties are too large and, as events have shown, the world still too unsettled for the United States to abandon its leadership role or the military power behind it. We have therefore reduced our military from the size necessary to fight the Cold War, but we have kept it at the size necessary to sustain our international leadership.

What I ask of you tonight is simply support for staying the course. This is no small thing. A properly focused, steady-as-you-go, more efficient defense policy requires just as much energy and imagination as any alternative. And persistence is a test of our character and our wisdom. We know from our own lives that finding the right path is half the job; the other half is to keep at it. Let it be said, therefore, of this generation of Americans that after winning the war, it knew how to win the peace.

BACKGROUND MATERIALS

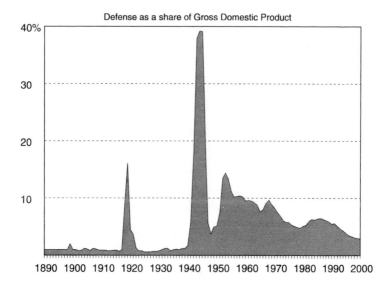

Fig. 1. Defense Spending and Gross Domestic Product, 1890–2000

SOURCES: Department of Defense and Office of Management and Budget.

Fig. 2. Defense Spending as a Share of Gross Domestic Product, 1960–2002

SOURCES: Department of Defense and Office of Management and Budget.

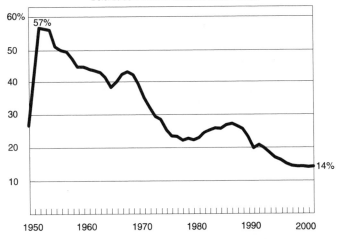

Defense as a share of Gross Domestic Product

Fig. 3. Defense Spending as a Share of Federal Outlays, 1950–2002

SOURCE: Department of Defense.

Budget Trends
(In FY 1997 constant dollars)

1985: $400 billion

-38%

1997: $250 billion

Manning Trends
(Number of active-duty personnel)

1985: 2.2 million

-33%

1997: 1.45 million
(Planned reduction to
1.36 million by 1999)

Fig. 4. Department of Defense Budget and Manning Trends

SOURCE: Department of Defense, *Quadrennial Defense Review* (1997).

[79]

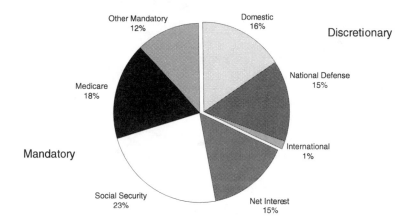

Fig. 5. Fiscal Year 1998 Federal Budget Requests

SOURCE: Center for Strategic and Budgetary Assessment.

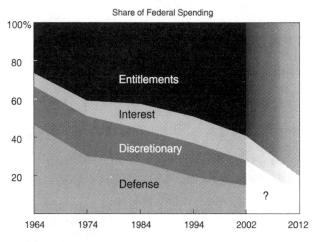

Fig. 6. The Coming Defense Squeeze

SOURCES: Congressional Budget Office, Department of Defense, and Office of Management and Budget.

Table 2. International Comparisons of Defense Expenditures and Defense Spending as a Percentage of Gross Domestic Product

(In millions of 1995 constant dollars)

	DEFENSE SPENDING 1985	DEFENSE SPENDING 1996	PERCENTAGE CHANGE	PERCENT OF GDP 1985	PERCENT OF GDP 1996
United States*	$400,000	$250,000	−38 ↓	6.2	3.4
Canada	10,688	8,387	−21.5↓	2.2	1.5
France	44,604	46,217	+3.6↑	4.0	3.1
Germany	48,149	38,432	−20.2↓	3.2	1.7
Turkey	3,134	6,856	+118.8↑	4.5	3.9
United Kingdom	43,536	32,764	−24.7↓	5.2	3.0
Soviet Union/Russia**	329,449	69,537	−78.9↓	16.1	6.5
Egypt	3,527	2,629	−25.4↓	7.2	4.5
Iran	19,423	3,301	−83 ↓	36.0	5.0
Iraq	17,573	1,224	−93 ↓	25.9	8.3
Israel	6,899	9,359	+35.7↑	21.2	12.1
Kuwait	2,453	3,505	+42.9↑	9.1	12.9
Saudi Arabia	24,530	16,999	−30.7↓	19.6	12.8
China	27,107	34,684	+27.9↑	7.9	5.7
India	8,553	10,158	+18.8↑	3.0	2.8
Japan	29,350	43,626	+48.6↑	1.0	1.0
North Korea	5,675	5,330	−6 ↓	23.0	27.2
South Korea	8,592	15,168	+76.5↑	5.1	3.3
Malaysia	2,409	3,542	+47 ↑	5.6	4.2
Pakistan	2,835	3,579	+26.2↑	6.9	5.7
Philippines	647	1,457	+125.2↑	1.4	2.0
Singapore	1,622	3,959	+144.1↑	6.7	5.5
Taiwan	8,793	13,297	+51.2↑	7.0	4.9
Argentina	4,945	3,732	−24.5↓	3.8	1.5
Brazil	3,209	10,341	+222.2↑	0.8	2.1
Chile	1,696	1,990	+17.3↑	7.8	3.5
Colombia	579	1,846	+218.8↑	1.6	2.6
Ecuador	388	528	+36.1↑	1.8	3.4
South Africa	3,922	2,506	−36.1↓	2.7	1.8

NOTE: *U.S. figures are in 1997 dollars. 1996 figures for U.S. represent fiscal year 1997.
**The Soviet Union in 1985 included many republics that are no longer part of Russia. These now-independent republics together spent $35,080 million on defense in 1996.

SOURCES: The International Institute for Strategic Studies, *1997/98 The Military Balance;* Department of Defense, *Quadrennial Defense Review* (1997).